PATRICIAN RHYMES

A RÉSUMÉ OF AMERICAN SOCIETY VERSE

PATRICIAN RHYMES

A RÉSUMÉ OF

AMERICAN SOCIETY VERSE

FROM PHILIP FRENEAU TO THE PRESENT DAY

EDITED WITH AN INTRODUCTION
BY
Clinton Scollard
AND
Jessie B. Rittenhouse

BOSTON AND NEW YORK
HOUGHTON MIFFLIN COMPANY
The Riverside Press Cambridge
1932

The Riverside Press
CAMBRIDGE · MASSACHUSETTS
PRINTED IN THE U.S.A.

ACKNOWLEDGMENTS

THANKS are due to the following publishers and authors for their kind permission to use the poems included in this volume:

The Bobbs-Merrill Company, for 'Valentine to One's Wife,' from *Sonata, and Other Poems*, by John Erskine, copyright, 1925, by special permission of the publishers, The Bobbs-Merrill Company.

The Century Company for 'Spades,' from *Bitter Brew*, and 'His Widow,' from *Stygian Freight*, by Cale Young Rice, copyright by the Century Company.

Covici, Friede, Inc., for 'To a Pretty Woman,' by J. U. Nicolson.

Dodd, Mead and Company, Inc., for 'Dinah Kneading Dough,' by Paul Laurence Dunbar, copyright, 1899, 1927, by Dodd, Mead and Company, Inc.

Doubleday, Doran and Company, Inc., for 'On a Child That Had Fever,' from *Poems* by Christopher Morley, copyright, 1929, by Doubleday, Doran and Company, Inc.; for 'Ballade to My Lady's Beauty,' from *Poems, Essays and Letters*, by Joyce Kilmer, copyright, 1914, 1917, 1918, by Doubleday, Doran and Company, Inc.; for 'As to Eyes,' from *In Other Words*, by Franklin P. Adams, copyright, 1912, by Doubleday, Doran and Company, Inc.; for 'To Lovers,' from *Se-*

lected Lyrics of Amelia Josephine Burr, copyright, 1927, by Doubleday, Doran and Company, Inc.; for 'Anne' and 'On a Colonial Picture,' from *The Selected Poems* of Lizette Woodworth Reese, copyright, 1926, by Doubleday, Doran and Company, Inc.

Duffield and Company for 'The Love of a Boy — Today,' from *Along the Trail*, by Richard Hovey.

Harper and Brothers, for 'To One Who Said Me Nay,' from *Color*, by Countee Cullen; for 'Song,' from *Poems*, by Dana Burnet; for 'This is She' and 'Fashion,' from *The Laughing Muse*, and 'A Plea,' from *The Light Guitar*, by Arthur Guiterman.

Henry Holt and Company, for 'The Rose Family,' from *West-Running Brook*, by Robert Frost.

Houghton Mifflin Company, for selections from the Collected Poems of Thomas Bailey Aldrich, Alice and Phœbe Cary, Richard Watson Gilder, Bret Harte, Oliver Wendell Holmes, Henry Wadsworth Longfellow, James Russell Lowell, Thomas William Parsons, John Godfrey Saxe, Edward Rowland Sill, William Wetmore Story, Frank Dempster Sherman, Edmund Clarence Stedman, Bayard Taylor, Maurice Thompson, and John Greenleaf Whittier; also for selections from the work of Anna Hempstead Branch, Helen Gray Cone, Margaret Deland, William Dean Howells, Elspeth MacDuffie O'Halloran, Jessie B. Rittenhouse, and Odell Shepard.

Harcourt, Brace and Company, for 'Warning' from *The Old Road to Paradise*, by Margaret Widdemer; for 'If You should Tire of Loving Me' and 'The Modern Woman to Her Lover,' from *Factories*, by Margaret

Widdemer, and for 'The Wise Woman' and 'The Embarrassed Amorist,' from *The New Adam*, by Louis Untermeyer.

Henry Harrison, for selections from the work of Ralph Cheney, Mary Carolyn Davies, and Lucia Trent.

Alfred A. Knopf, Inc., for 'The Coquette,' 'The Skeptic,' and 'To No One in Particular,' by Witter Bynner, reprinted from *Grenstone Poems* by and with permission of and special arrangement with Alfred A. Knopf, Inc., authorized publishers; and for 'A Modern Lochinvar,' from *A Ghost in the Attic*, by George S. Bryan.

Horace Liveright, for 'Let Our Love Be,' from *Poems in Praise of Practically Nothing*, by Samuel Hoffenstein.

The Macmillan Company, for selections from the work of John Kendrick Bangs, Alice Brown, Orrick Johns, Percy MacKaye, and Sara Teasdale.

Charles Scribner's Sons, for selections from *The Complete Poems* of Sidney Lanier, Henry Cuyler Bunner, and from the work of Oliver Herford, Edward Sanford Martin, and Charles Henry Luders.

The Southwest Press, for 'I Gave my Love,' from *Red Heels*, by Lexie Dean Robertson.

The Viking Press, Inc., for 'Vows' and 'Battery Park,' by Leonard Cline, from *After-Walker*.

Yale University Press, for 'Love's Detective' and 'Can't,' from *Shadow Verses*, by Gamaliel Bradford.

The Editors wish to thank personally the following poets who have graciously given special permission for the use of copyrighted material: Franklin P. Adams,

Kendall Banning, Gamaliel Bradford, Anna Hempstead Branch, Alice Brown, George S. Bryan, Gelett Burgess, Dana Burnet, Amelia Josephine Burr, Richard Burton, Witter Bynner, Francis Carlin, Ralph Cheney, Arthur Colton, Helen Gray Cone, Countee Cullen, Mary Carolyn Davies, Charles Divine, John Erksine, John Farrar, Robert Frost, Theodosia Garrison, William Griffith, Edwin Osgood Grover, Arthur Guiterman, Gertrude Hall, Samuel Hoffenstein, Louis How, Robert Underwood Johnson, Thomas S. Jones, Jr., Harry Kemp, Arthur Ketchum, Virginia Lawrence, Mary Sinton Leitch, Percy MacKaye, Edward Sanford Martin, Edna St. Vincent Millay, John Richard Moreland, Harrison Smith Morris, J. U. Nicolson, Elspeth Mac-Duffie O'Halloran, Dorothy Parker, Samuel Minturn Peck, Frederick Peterson, Ezra Pound, Lizette Woodworth Reese, Cale Young Rice, Lexie Dean Robertson, Sidney King Russell, Odell Shepard, Sara Teasdale, Charles Hanson Towne, Lucia Trent, Louis Untermeyer, Harold Vinal, Willard Wattles, Carolyn Wells, John Hall Wheelock, and Margaret Widdemer.

CONTENTS

xi

xiv

INTRODUCTION

D URING *an after-dinner talk, many years ago, at the home of the artist-poet Christopher P. Cranch, the subject of American light verse came up for discussion. Mrs. Cranch, at her husband's suggestion, produced from among her treasures some lines which her uncle, John Quincy Adams, had addressed to her while she was yet a girl. Mr. Cranch read them. They danced and tripped and sparkled. They evoked a smile. 'Yes,' Mr. Cranch declared, as he concluded, 'despite Freneau's one charming adventure in this field, John Quincy Adams was the first American to strike the Society Verse note.'. Mr. Cranch was right. While there may be isolated examples of light verse prior to this period it was our sixth President who, consciously or unconsciously, was the earliest American to employ the distinctive type of poetry which has been called Vers de Société. Erudite although he was, weighty as his polemics and state papers may be, he had, upon occasion, a nimbleness of fancy and a smiling turn of phrase. John Quincy Adams was, with us, the father of Patrician Rhymes. He must have sat at the feet of Goldsmith and that strange, half-mad recluse of Olney, Cowper, and had he not been so engrossed with public affairs he might have endeared himself to his countrymen quite as much as a poet as he did as a statesman.*

*Vers de Société, Society Verse, Familiar Verse, Occasional Verse, Lyra Elegantiarum, Patrician Rhymes —
these are some of the designations of the type of poetry we
are considering. Perfect examples of it, like Ben Jonson's
'Drink to me only with thine Eyes' and Lovelace's 'To
Lucasta on Going to the Wars,' have outlasted scores of
ponderous epics. We shall let two accomplished expositors
of the art explain its fine distinctions.*

*'It should be,' Frederick Locker declares, 'short, elegant,
refined and fanciful, not seldom distinguished by chastened
sentiment, and often playful. The rhythm should be crisp
and sparkling, and the rhyme never forced, while the entire
poem should be marked by tasteful moderation, high finish
and completeness.' Again avers Mr. Locker: 'The poem
may be tinctured with a well-bred philosophy, it may be gay
and gallant, it may even be trifling, but it must never be
heavy or commonplace.'*

*In the opinion of Edmund Clarence Stedman 'true Vers
de Société is marked by humor, by spontaneity, joined with
extreme elegance of finish, by the quality we call breeding,
— above all by lightness of touch.'*

*We find a trace of the Society Verse mood in the Greek
Anthology. It shows itself distinctly in the poetry of
Horace and Catullus. It is present in the work of some of
the Troubadours. It flashes out in not a few of the earlier
and later French lyrists, and it is seen in certain songs of
Heine. If we would seek for the earliest example of Patrician Rhymes in English we must go back to the fifteenth
century and the curious, whimsical, and occasionally ribald
John Skelton. Among the Elizabethans we discover the*

Society Verse note not infrequently sounded, witness Lyly, Sidney, Shakespeare, and Ben Jonson. But it was the blithe cavaliers, 'the sons of Ben,' as they were wont to call themselves, who developed to the full this type of poetry. What a gallant group they were, and how they made the court of the first James and that of the unfortunate first Charles ring with their songs! What a galaxy of names — Wither, Herrick, Carew, Suckling, Lovelace, Habington! Then later came Waller and the reckless roué Rochester. Not long after the dawn of the eighteenth century appeared the accomplished Prior and Gay of the 'Fables' and 'Beggar's Opera,' to be joined by the staid Gray of 'Elegy' fame. These were followed by Cowper and Goldsmith. In the nineteenth century Praed, Locker, and Dobson gave to Society Verse its modern flavor.

Passing in review our own Patrician Rhymes of more than one hundred years, it is well to bear in mind that much which was pertinent in the past would not be so regarded now, and yet, though the fashion of verse may change, the dominant impulses of man remain unaltered.

'One of the most notable specimens of Vers de Société in any language is Pope's "Rape of the Lock,"' declares Frederick Locker, and yet Mr. Locker, on account of its length, did not include this poem in his comprehensive collection, Lyra Elegantiarum. The same objection might be urged against the use in this volume of Butler's 'Nothing to Wear.' However, this piece is so palpably in the vein of this collection that it seems desirable to include it. In a résumé of American Society Verse it has a distinct place.

It is inevitable, when so many have adventured into this

field, that some writers of American light verse would be omitted, yet we trust that the representation within these pages is adequate. The exigencies of copyright have, however, curtailed examples from the work of some of our recent fashioners of Patrician Rhymes.

THE EDITORS

PATRICIAN RHYMES

SONG OF THYRSIS

THE turtle on yon withered bough,
That lately mourned her murdered mate,
Has found another comrade now —
Such changes all await!
Again her drooping plume is drest,
Again she's willing to be blest
And takes her lover to her nest.

If nature has decreed it so
With all above, and all below,
Let us like them forget our woe,
    And not be killed with sorrow.
If I should quit your arms tonight
And chance to die before 'twas light,
I would advise you — and you might —
    Love again tomorrow.

                                    PHILIP FRENEAU

THE LIP AND THE HEART

ONE day between the Lip and Heart
    A wordless strife arose,
Which was expertest in the art
    His purpose to disclose.

3

The Lip called forth the vassal Tongue
  And made him vouch — a lie!
The slave his servile anthem sung,
  And braved the listening sky.

The Heart to speak in vain essayed,
  Nor could his purpose reach —
His will nor voice nor tongue obeyed,
  His silence was his speech.

Mark thou their difference, child of earth!
  While each performs his part,
Not all the Lip can speak is worth
  The silence of the Heart.

                              JOHN QUINCY ADAMS

TO SALLY

THE man in righteousness arrayed,
  A pure and blameless liver,
Needs not the keen Toledo blade,
  Nor venom-freighted quiver.
What though he wind his toilsome way
  O'er regions wild and weary —
Through Zara's burning desert stray,
  Or Asia's jungles dreary:

What though he plow the billowy deep
  By lunar light, or solar,

4

Meet the resistless Simoon's sweep,
 Or iceberg circumpolar!
In bog or quagmire deep and dank
 His foot shall never settle;
He mounts the summit of Mount Blanc,
 Or Popocatepetl.

On Chimborazo's breathless height
 He treads o'er burning lava;
Or snuffs the Bohan Upas blight,
 The deathful plant of Java.
Through every peril he shall pass,
 By Virtue's shield protected;
And still by Truth's unerring glass
 His path shall be directed.

Else wherefore was it, Thursday last,
 While strolling down the valley,
Defenceless, musing as I passed
 A canzonet to Sally,
A wolf, with mouth-protruding snout,
 Forth from his thicket bounded —
I clapped my hands and raised a shout —
 He heard — and fled — confounded.

Tangier nor Tunis never bred
 An animal more crabbed;
Nor Fez, dry-nurse of lions, fed
 A monster half so rabid;

Nor Ararat so fierce a beast
    Has seen since days of Noah;
Nor stronger, eager for a feast,
    The fell constrictor boa.

Oh! place me where the solar beam
    Has scorched all verdure vernal;
Or on the polar verge extreme,
    Blocked up with ice eternal —
Still shall my voice's tender lays
    Of love remain unbroken;
And still my charming Sally praise,
    Sweet smiling and sweet spoken.

                    JOHN QUINCY ADAMS

THE WANTS OF MAN

(EXTRACT)

'MAN wants but little here below,
    Nor wants that little long.'
'Tis not with me exactly so,
    But 'tis so in the song.
My wants are many, and if told
    Would muster many a score;
And were each wish a mint of gold,
    I still should long for more.

What first I want is daily bread,
    And canvas-backs and wine;

6

And all the realms of nature spread
    Before me when I dine.
Four courses scarcely can provide
    My appetite to quell,
With four choice cooks from France, beside,
    To dress my dinner well.

And then I want a mansion fair,
    A dwelling house in style,
Four stories high, for wholesome air —
    A massive marble pile;
With halls for banquets and for balls,
    All furnished rich and fine;
With stabled studs in fifty stalls,
    And cellars for my wine.

I want a garden and a park,
    My dwelling to surround —
A thousand acres (bless the mark!)
    With walls encompassed round —
Where flocks may range and herds may low,
    And kids and lambkins play,
And flowers and fruits commingled grow,
    All Eden to display.

I want, when summer's foliage falls,
    And autumn strips the trees,
A house within the city walls,
    For comfort and for ease.

But here, as space is somewhat scant,
   And acres somewhat rare,
My house in town I only want
   To occupy — a square!

I want a steward, butler, cooks;
   A coachman, footman, grooms,
A library of well-bound books,
   And picture-garnished rooms;
Correggios, Magdalen and Night,
   The Matron of the Chair;
Guido's fleet coursers in their flight,
   And Claudes at least a pair.

I want a board of burnished plate,
   Of silver and of gold;
Tureens of twenty pounds in weight,
   With sculpture's richest mould;
Plateaus, with chandeliers and lamps,
   Plates, dishes — all the same;
And porcelain vases, with the stamps
   Of Sèvres, Angoulême.

And maples, of the finest stain,
   Must form my chamber doors,
And carpets of the Milton grain
   Must cover all my floors;
My walls, with tapestry bedecked,
   Must never be outdone;

And damask curtains must protect
  Their colors from the sun.

And mirrors of the largest pane'
  From Venice must be brought;
And sandalwood, and bamboo cane,
  For chairs and tables bought;
On all the mantel-pieces clocks
  Of thrice-gilt bronze must stand,
And screens of ebony and box
  Invite the stranger's hand.

I want (who does not want?) a wife,
  Affectionate and fair,
To solace all the woes of life,
  And all its joys to share;
Of temper sweet, of yielding will,
  Of firm yet placid mind,
With all my faults to love me still,
  With sentiment refined.

And as Time's car incessant runs,
  And fortune fills my store,
I want of daughters and of sons
  From eight to half a score.
I want (alas! can mortal dare
  Such bliss on earth to crave?)
That all the girls be chaste and fair —
  The boys all wise and brave.

JOHN QUINCY ADAMS

SONG

WHO has robbed the ocean cave
   To tinge thy lips with coral hue?
Who from India's distant wave
   For thee those pearly treasures drew?
      Who, from yonder orient sky,
      Stole the morning of thine eye?

Thousand charms, thy form to deck,
   From sea and earth and air are torn;
Roses bloom upon thy cheek,
   On thy breath their fragrance borne.
      Guard thy bosom from the day
      Lest thy snows should melt away.

But one charm remains behind,
   Which mute earth can ne'er impart;
Nor in ocean wilt thou find
   Nor in circling air a heart.
      Fairest, would'st thou perfect be,
      Take, oh, take that heart from me!

JOHN SHAW

A CERTAIN YOUNG LADY

THERE'S a certain young lady,
Who's just in her heyday,
   And full of all mischief, I ween;

10

So teasing! so pleasing!
Capricious! delicious!
And you know very well whom I mean.

With an eye dark as night,
Yet than noonday more bright,
   Was ever a black eye so keen?
      It can thrill with a glance,
      With a beam can entrance,
   And you know very well whom I mean.

With a stately step — such as
You'd expect in a duchess —
   And a brow might distinguish a queen,
      With a mighty proud air,
      That says 'touch me who dare,'
   And you know very well whom I mean.

With a toss of the head
That strikes one quite dead,
   But a smile to revive one again;
      That toss so appalling!
      That smile so enthralling!
   And you know very well whom I mean.

Confound her! devil take her! —
A cruel heart-breaker —
   But hold! see that smile so serene!
      God love her! God bless her!

May nothing distress her!
You know very well whom I mean.

Heaven help the adorer
Who happens to bore her,
The lover who wakens her spleen!
But too blest for a sinner
Is he who shall win her,
And you know very well whom I mean.

WASHINGTON IRVING

WOMAN

LADY, although we have not met,
And may not meet, beneath the sky;
And whether thine are eyes of jet,
Gray, or dark blue, or violet,
Or hazel — Heaven knows, not I;

Whether around thy cheek of rose
A maiden's glowing locks are curled,
And to some thousand kneeling beaux
Thy frown is cold as winter's snows,
Thy smile is worth a world;

Or whether, past youth's joyous strife,
The calm of thought is on thy brow,
And thou art in thy noon of life,
Loving and loved, a happy wife,
And happier mother now —

I know not: but, whate'er thou art,
  Whoe'er thou art, were mine the spell
To call Fate's joys or blunt his dart,
There should not be one hand or heart
  But served or wished thee well.

For thou art woman — with that word
  Life's dearest hopes and memories come,
Truth, Beauty, Love — in her adored,
And earth's lost Paradise restored
  In the green bower of home.

What is man's love? His vows are broke
  Even while his parting kiss is warm;
But woman's love all change will mock,
And, like the ivy round the oak,
  Cling closest in the storm.

And well the Poet at her shrine
  May bend, and worship while he woos;
To him she is a thing divine,
The inspiration of his line,
  His Sweetheart and his Muse.

If to his song the echo rings
  Of Fame — 'tis woman's voice he hears;
If ever from his lyre's proud strings
Flow sounds like rush of angel-wings,
'Tis that she listens while he sings,
  With blended smiles and tears:

Smiles — tears — whose blessed and blessing
       power
   Like sun and dew o'er summer's tree,
Alone keeps green through Time's long hour,
That frailer thing than leaf or flower,
   A poet's immortality.

FITZ-GREENE HALLECK

INCONSTANCY

YES! I swore to be true, I allow,
   And I meant it, but somehow or other,
The seal of that amorous vow
   Was pressed on the lips of another.

Yet I did but as all would have done,
   For where is the being, dear cousin,
Content with the beauties of one
   When he might have the range of a dozen?

Young Love is a changeable boy,
   And the gem of the sea-rock is like him,
For he gives back the beams of his joy
   To each sunny eye that may strike him.

From a kiss of a zephyr and rose
   Love sprang in an exquisite hour,
And fleeting and sweet, heaven knows,
   Is this child of a sigh and a flower.

JOSEPH RODMAN DRAKE

IF I COULD LOVE

If I could love, I'd find me out
  A roguish, laughing eye,
A cheek to blush, a lip to pout,
  A pure, kind heart to sigh;

A fairy hand to touch and glance
  From note to note with glee,
A fairy foot to trip the dance
  And lead it down with me;

A soul to share in all my fun
  And feel for all my woes,
And as our little life should run
  To take it as it goes;

And O, when follies all have fled
  And solemn thoughts shall rise,
To soothe me on my dying bed
  And meet me in the skies;

Such thoughts are vain, too vain — yet why
  Should you my thoughts reprove —
O pity, pity me, for I
  Am poor, and cannot love!

JOHN GARDNER CALKINS BRAINARD

SERENADE

Look out upon the stars, my love,
    And shame them with thine eyes,
On which, than on the lights above,
    There hang more destinies.
Night's beauty is the harmony
    Of blending shades and light:
Then, lady, up, — look out, and be
    A sister to the night.

Sleep not! — thine image wakes for aye
    Within my watching breast;
Sleep not! — from her soft sleep should fly,
    Who robs all hearts of rest.
Nay, lady, from thy slumbers break,
    And make this darkness gay,
With looks whose brightness well might make
    Of darker nights a day.

EDWARD COATE PINKNEY

A HEALTH

I fill this cup to one made up
    Of loveliness alone,
A woman, of her gentle sex
    The seeming paragon;
To whom the better elements
    And kindly stars have given

16

A form so fair, that, like the air,
   'Tis less of earth than heaven.

Her every tone is music's own,
   Like those of morning birds,
And something more than melody
   Dwells ever in her words;
The coinage of her heart are they,
   And from her lips each flows
As one may see the burdened bee
   Forth issue from the rose.

Affections are as thoughts to her,
   The measures of her hours;
Her feelings have the fragrancy,
   The freshness of young flowers;
And lovely passions, changing oft,
   So fill her, she appears
The image of themselves by turns,—
   The idol of past years!

Of her bright face one glance will trace
   A picture on the brain,
And of her voice in echoing hearts
   A sound must long remain;
But memory, such as mine of her,
   So very much endears,
When death is nigh my latest sigh
   Will not be life's, but hers.

I fill this cup to one made up
  Of loveliness alone,
A woman, of her gentle sex
  The seeming paragon —
Her health! and would on earth there stood
  Some more of such a frame,
That life might all be poetry,
  And weariness a name.

EDWARD COATE PINKNEY

A SONG

WE break the glass, whose sacred wine
  To some belovèd health we drain,
Lest future pledges, less divine,
  Should e'er the hallowed toy profane;
And thus I broke a heart that poured
  Its tide of feelings out for thee,
In draughts, by after-times deplored,
  Yet dear to memory.

But still the old, impassioned ways
  And habits of my mind remain,
And still unhappy light displays
  Thine image chambered in my brain,
And still it looks as when the hours
  Went by like flights of singing birds,
Or that soft chain of spoken flowers
  And airy gems, — thy words.

EDWARD COATE PINKNEY

LOVE IN A COTTAGE

THEY may talk of love in a cottage,
  And bowers of trellised vine, —
Of nature bewitchingly simple,
  And milkmaids half divine;
They may talk of the pleasure of sleeping
  In the shade of a spreading tree,
And a walk in the fields at morning
  By the side of a footstep free.

But give me a sly flirtation
  By the light of a chandelier,
With music to play in the pauses,
  And nobody very near;
Or a seat on a silken sofa,
  With a glass of pure old wine,
And mamma too blind to discover
  The small white hand in mine.

Your love in a cottage is hungry,
  Your vine is a nest for flies,
Your milkmaid shocks the Graces,
  And simplicity talks of pies.
You lie down to your shady slumber
  And wake with a bug in your ear,
And your damsel that walks in the morning
  Is shod like a mountaineer.

True love is at home on a carpet,
  And mightily likes his ease,

And true love has an eye for dinner,
　And starves beneath shady trees.
His wing is the fan of a lady,
　His foot's an invisible thing,
And his arrow is tipped with a jewel
　And shot from a silver string.

NATHANIEL PARKER WILLIS

TO HELEN IN A HUFF

NAY, lady, one frown is enough
　In a life as soon over as this —
And though minutes seem long in a huff,
　They're minutes 'tis pity to miss!
The smiles you imprison so lightly
　Are reckoned, like days in eclipse;
And though you may smile again brightly,
　You've lost so much light from your lips!
　　Pray, lady, smile!

The cup that is longest untasted
　May be with our bliss running o'er,
And, love when we will, we have wasted
　An age in not loving before!
Perchance Cupid's forging a fetter
　To tie us together some day,
And, just for the chance, we had better
　Be laying up love, I should say!
　　Nay, lady, smile!

NATHANIEL PARKER WILLIS

L'AMOUR SANS AILES

Young Love, when tender mood beset him,
  One morn to Lilla's casement flew,
Who raised it just so far to let him
  Blow half his fragrant kisses through.

Love brought no perch on which to rest,
  And Lilla had not one to give him,
And now she thought, her soul distressed, —
  What should she do? where would she leave him?

Love maddens to be thus half caught,
  His struggle Lilla's pain increases;
'He'll fly — he'll fly away,' she thought,
  'Or beat himself and wings to pieces.

'His wings — why them I do not want —
  The restless things make all this pother;'
Love tries to fly, but finds he can't,
  And nestles near her like a brother.

Plumeless, we call him *Friendship* now;
  Love smiles at acting such a part —
But what cares he for lover's vow
  While thus *perdu* near Lilla's heart!

                         CHARLES FENNO HOFFMAN

THE RETORT

Old Nick, who taught the village school,
   Wedded a maid of homespun habit;
He was as stubborn as a mule,
   She was as playful as a rabbit.

Poor Jane had scarce become a wife,
   Before her husband sought to make her
The pink of country-polished life,
   And prim and formal as a Quaker.

One day the tutor went abroad,
   And simple Jennie sadly missed him;
When he returned, behind her lord
   She shyly stole, and fondly kissed him.

The husband's anger rose — and red
   And white his face alternate grew!
'Less freedom, ma'am!'.... Jane sighed and said,
   'Oh, dear! I didn't know 'twas you!'

GEORGE POPE MORRIS

BEWARE

(Translated from the German

I know a maiden fair to see,
   Take care!
She can both false and friendly be,
   Beware! Beware!
   Trust her not,
   She is fooling thee!

She has two eyes, so soft and brown,
    Take care!
She gives a side-glance and looks down,
    Beware! Beware!
    Trust her not,
She is fooling thee!

And she has hair of a golden hue,
    Take care!
And what she says, it is not true,
    Beware! Beware!
    Trust her not,
She is fooling thee!

She has a bosom as white as snow,
    Take care!
She knows how much it is best to show,
    Beware! Beware!
    Trust her not,
She is fooling thee!

She gives thee a garland woven fair,
    Take care!
It is a fool's-cap for thee to wear,
    Beware! Beware!
    Trust her not,
She is fooling thee!
                    HENRY WADSWORTH LONGFELLOW

23

THE HENCHMAN

My LADY walks her morning round,
My lady's page her fleet greyhound,
My lady's hair the fond winds stir,
And all the birds make songs for her.

Her thrushes sing in Rathburn bowers,
And Rathburn side is gay with flowers;
But ne'er like hers, in flower or bird,
Was beauty seen or music heard.

The distance of the stars is hers;
The least of all her worshippers,
The dust beneath her dainty heel,
She knows not that I see or feel.

Oh, proud and calm! — she cannot know
Where'er she goes with her I go;
Oh, cold and fair! — she cannot guess
I kneel to share her hound's caress!

Gay knights beside her hunt and hawk,
I rob their ears of her sweet talk;
Her suitors come from east and west,
I steal her smiles from every guest.

Unheard of her, in loving words,
I greet her with the song of birds;
I reach her with her green-armed bowers,
I kiss her with the lips of flowers.

The hound and I are on her trail,
The wind and I uplift her veil;
As if the calm, cold moon she were,
And I the tide, I follow her.

As unrebuked as they, I share
The license of the sun and air,
And in a common homage hide
My worship from her scorn and pride.

World-wide apart, and yet so near,
I breathe her charmèd atmosphere,
Wherein to her my service brings
The reverence due to holy things.

Her maiden pride, her haughty name,
My dumb devotion shall not shame;
The love that no return doth crave
To knightly levels lifts the slave.

No lance have I, in joust or fight,
To splinter in my lady's sight;
But at her feet, how blest were I
For any need of hers to die!

JOHN GREENLEAF WHITTIER

THE DILEMMA

Now, by the blessed Paphian queen,
Who heaves the breast of sweet sixteen;
By every name I cut on bark
Before my morning star grew dark;

By Hymen's torch, by Cupid's dart,
By all that thrills the beating heart;
The bright black eye, the melting blue, —
I cannot choose between the two.

I had a vision in my dreams; —
I saw a row of twenty beams;
From every beam a rope was hung,
In every rope a lover swung;
I asked the hue of every eye
That bade each luckless lover die;
Ten shadowy lips said, heavenly blue,
And ten accused the darker hue.

I asked a matron which she deemed
With fairest light of beauty beamed;
She answered, some thought both were fair, —
Give her blue eyes and golden hair.
I might have liked her judgment well,
But, as she spoke, she rang the bell,
And all her girls, nor small nor few,
Came marching in, — their eyes were blue.

I asked a maiden; back she flung
The locks that round her forehead hung,
And turned her eye, a glorious one,
Bright as a diamond in the sun,
On me, until beneath its rays
I felt as if my hair would blaze;
She liked all eyes but eyes of green;
She looked at me; what could she mean?

26

Ah! many lids Love lurks between,
Nor heeds the coloring of his screen;
And when his random arrows fly,
The victim falls, but knows not why.
Gaze not upon his shield of jet,
The shaft upon the string is set;
Look not beneath his azure veil,
Though every limb were cased in mail.

Well, both might make a martyr break
The chain that bound him to the stake;
And both, with but a single ray,
Can melt our very hearts away;
And both, when balanced, hardly seem
To stir the scales, or rock the beam;
But that is dearest, all the while,
That wears for us the sweetest smile.

OLIVER WENDELL HOLMES

MY AUNT

My AUNT! my dear unmarried aunt!
    Long years have o'er her flown;
Yet still she strains the aching clasp
    That binds her virgin zone;
I know it hurts her, — though she looks
    As cheerful as she can;
Her waist is ampler than her life,
    For life is but a span.

27

My aunt! my poor deluded aunt!
   Her hair is almost gray;
Why will she train that winter curl
   In such a spring-like way?
How can she lay her glasses down,
   And say she reads as well,
When, through a double convex lens,
   She just makes out to spell?

Her father — grandpapa! forgive
   This erring lip its smiles —
Vowed she should make the finest girl
   Within a hundred miles;
He sent her to a stylish school;
   'Twas in her thirteenth June;
And with her, as the rules required,
   'Two towels and a spoon.'

They braced my aunt against a board,
   To make her straight and tall;
They laced her up, they starved her down,
   To make her light and small;
They pinched her feet, they singed her hair,
   They screwed it up with pins; —
O never mortal suffered more
   In penance for her sins.

So, when my precious aunt was done,
   My grandsire brought her back;
(By daylight, lest some rabid youth
   Might follow on the track;)

'Ah!' said my grandsire, as he shook
   Some powder in his pan,
'What could this lovely creature do
   Against a desperate man!'

Alas! nor chariot, nor barouche,
   Nor bandit cavalcade,
Tore from the trembling father's arms
   His all-accomplished maid.
For her how happy had it been!
   And Heaven had spared to me
To see one sad, ungathered rose
   On my ancestral tree.

OLIVER WENDELL HOLMES

THE LAST LEAF

I saw him once before,
As he passed by the door,
   And again
The pavement stones resound,
As he totters o'er the ground
   With his cane.

They say that in his prime,
Ere the pruning-knife of Time
   Cut him down,
Not a better man was found
By the Crier on his round
   Through the town.

But now he walks the streets,
And he looks at all he meets
    Sad and wan,
And he shakes his feeble head,
That seems as if he said,
    'They are gone.'

The mossy marbles rest
On the lips that he has prest
    In their bloom,
And the names he loved to hear
Have been carved for many a year
    On the tomb.

My grandmamma has said —
Poor old lady, she is dead
    Long ago, —
That he had a Roman nose,
And his cheek was like a rose
    In the snow.

But now his nose is thin,
And it rests upon his chin
    Like a staff,
And a crook is in his back,
And a melancholy crack
    In his laugh.

I know it is a sin
For me to sit and grin
    At him here;

But the old three-cornered hat,
And the breeches, and all that,
   Are so queer!

And if I should live to be
The last leaf upon the tree
   In the spring, —
Let them smile, as I do now,
At the old forsaken bough
   Where I cling.

OLIVER WENDELL HOLMES

CONTENTMENT

LITTLE I ask; my wants are few;
   I only wish a hut of stone,
(A *very plain* brown stone will do,)
   That I may call my own; —
And close at hand is such a one,
In yonder street that fronts the sun.

Plain food is quite enough for me;
   Three courses are as good as ten; —
If Nature can subsist on three,
   Thank Heaven for three. Amen!
I always thought cold victuals nice; —
My *choice* would be vanilla-ice.

I care not much for gold or land; —
   Give me a mortgage here and there, —

Some good bank-stock, — some note of hand,
    Or trifling railroad share, —
I only ask that Fortune send
A *little* more than I shall spend.

Honors are silly toys, I know,
    And titles are but empty names;
I would, *perhaps*, be Plenipo, —
    But only near St. James;
I'm very sure I should not care
To fill our Gubernator's chair.

Jewels are baubles; 'tis a sin
    To care for such unfruitful things; —
One good-sized diamond in a pin, —
    Some, *not so large*, in rings, —
A ruby, and a pearl, or so,
Will do for me; — I laugh at show.

My dame should dress in cheap attire;
    (Good, heavy silks are never dear;) —
I own perhaps I *might* desire
    Some shawls of true Cashmere, —
Some marrowy crapes of China silk,
Like wrinkled skins on scalded milk.

I would not have the horse I drive
    So fast that folks must stop and stare;
An easy gait — two, forty-five —
    Suits me; I do not care; —

Perhaps, for just a *single spurt*,
Some seconds less would do no hurt.

Of pictures, I should like to own
   Titians and Raphaels three or four, —
I love so much their style and tone, —
   One Turner, and no more,
(A landscape, — foreground golden dirt, —
 The sunshine painted with a squirt.)

Of books but few, — some fifty score
   For daily use, and bound for wear;
The rest upon an upper floor; —
   Some *little* luxury *there*
Of red morocco's gilded gleam,
And vellum rich as country cream.

Busts, cameos, gems, — such things as these,
   Which others often show for pride,
I value for their power to please,
   And selfish churls deride; —
One Stradivarius, I confess,
Two Meerschaums, I would fain possess.

Wealth's wasteful tricks I will not learn,
   Nor ape the glittering upstart fool; —
Shall not carved tables serve my turn,
   But *all* must be of buhl?
Give grasping pomp its double share, —
I ask but one recumbent chair.

33

Thus humble let me live and die,
    Nor long for Midas' golden touch;
If Heaven more generous gifts deny,
    I shall not miss them much, —
Too grateful for the blessing lent
Of simple tastes and mind content.

OLIVER WENDELL HOLMES

MABEL, IN NEW HAMPSHIRE

FAIREST of the fairest, rival of the rose,
That is Mabel of the Hills, as everybody knows.

Do you ask me near what stream this sweet floweret
        grows?
That's an ignorant question, sir, as everybody knows.

Ask you what her age is, reckoned as time goes?
Just the age of beauty, as everybody knows.

Is she tall as Rosalind, standing on her toes?
She is just the perfect height, as everybody knows.

What's the color of her eyes, when they ope or close?
Just the color they should be, as everybody knows.

Is she lovelier dancing, or resting in repose?
Both are radiant pictures, as everybody knows.

Do her ships go sailing on every wind that blows?
She is richer far than that, as everybody knows.

34

Has she scores of lovers, heaps of bleeding beaux?
That question's quite superfluous, as everybody knows.

I could tell you something, if I only chose! —
But what's the use of telling what everybody knows?

JAMES T. FIELDS

EARLY RISING

'GOD bless the man who first invented sleep!'
    So Sancho Panza said, and so say I:
And bless him also that he didn't keep
    His great discovery to himself; nor try
To make it — as the lucky fellow might —
A close monopoly by patent-right.

Yes — bless the man who first invented sleep,
    (I really can't avoid the iteration;)
But blast the man, with curses loud and deep,
    Whate'er the rascal's name, or age, or station,
Who first invented, and went round advising,
That artificial cut-off — Early Rising!

'Rise with the lark, and with the lark to bed,'
    Observes some solemn, sentimental owl;
Maxims like these are very cheaply said;
    But, ere you make yourself a fool or fowl,
Pray just inquire about his rise and fall,
And whether larks have any beds at all!

35

The time for honest folks to be a-bed
  Is in the morning, if I reason right;
And he who cannot keep his precious head
  Upon his pillow till it's fairly light,
And so enjoy his forty morning winks,
Is up to knavery; or else — he drinks!

Thompson, who sang about the 'Seasons,' said
  It was a glorious thing to *rise* in season;
But then he said it — lying — in his bed,
  At ten o'clock A. M.,— the very reason
He wrote so charmingly. The simple fact is
His preaching wasn't sanctioned by his practice.

'Tis, doubtless, well to be sometimes awake, —
  Awake to duty and awake to truth, —
But when, alas! a nice review we take
  Of our best deeds and days, we find, in sooth,
The hours that leave the slightest cause to weep
Are those we passed in childhood or asleep!

'Tis beautiful to leave the world awhile
  For the soft visions of the gentle night;
And free, at last, from mortal care or guile,
  To live as only in the angels' sight,
In sleep's sweet realm so cosily shut in,
Where, at the worst, we only *dream* of sin!

So let us sleep, and give the Maker praise.
  I like the lad who, when his father thought

To clip his morning nap by hackneyed phrase
  Of vagrant worm by early songster caught,
Cried, 'Served him right! — it's not at all surprising;
The worm was punished, sir, for early rising!'

JOHN GODFREY SAXE

MY FAMILIAR

AGAIN I hear that creaking step! —
    He's rapping at the door! —
Too well I know the boding sound
    That ushers in a bore.
I do not tremble when I meet
    The stoutest of my foes,
But Heaven defend me from the friend
    Who comes — but never goes!

He drops into my easy-chair,
    And asks about the news;
He peers into my manuscript,
    And gives his candid views;
He tells me where he likes the line,
    And where he's forced to grieve;
He takes the strangest liberties, —
    But never takes his leave!

He reads my daily paper through
    Before I've seen a word;
He scans the lyric (that I wrote)
    And thinks it quite absurd;

37

He calmly smokes my last cigar,
  And coolly asks for more;
He opens everything he sees —
  Except the entry door!

He talks about his fragile health,
  And tells me of the pains
He suffers from a score of ills
  Of which he ne'er complains;
And how he struggled once with death
  To keep the fiend at bay;
On themes like those away he goes, —
  But never goes away!

He tells me of the carping words
  Some shallow critic wrote;
And every precious paragraph
  Familiarly can quote;
He thinks the writer did me wrong;
  He'd like to run him through!
He says a thousand pleasant things, —
  But never says, 'Adieu!'

Whene'er he comes, — that dreadful man, —
  Disguise it as I may,
I know that, like an autumn rain,
  He'll last throughout the day.
In vain I speak of urgent tasks;
  In vain I scowl and pout;

A frown is no extinguisher, —
     It does not put him out!

I mean to take the knocker off,
     Put crape upon the door,
Or hint to John that I am gone
     To stay a month or more.
I do not tremble when I meet
     The stoutest of my foes,
But Heaven defend me from the friend
     Who never, never goes!

JOHN GODFREY SAXE

THE COQUETTE

'You're clever at drawing, I own,'
     Said my beautiful cousin Lisette,
As we sat by the window alone,
     'But say, can you paint a Coquette?'

'She's painted already,' quoth I;
     'Nay, nay!' said the laughing Lisette,
'Now none of your joking — but try
     And paint me a thorough Coquette.'

'Well, Cousin,' at once I began
     In the ear of the eager Lisette,
'I'll paint you as well as I can,
     That wonderful thing, a Coquette.

'She wears a most beautiful face'
  ('Of course,' said the pretty Lisette),
'And isn't deficient in grace,
  Or else she were not a Coquette.

'And then she is daintily made'
  (A smile from the dainty Lisette)
'By people expert in the trade
  Of forming a proper Coquette.

'She's the winningest ways with the beaux'
  ('Go on!' said the winning Lisette),
'But there isn't a man of them knows
  The mind of the fickle Coquette!

'She knows how to weep and to sigh'
  (A sigh from the tender Lisette),
'But her weeping is all in my eye —
  Not that of the cunning Coquette!

'In short, she's a creature of art'
  ('Oh, hush!' said the frowning Lisette),
'With merely the ghost of a heart —
  Enough for a thorough Coquette.

'And yet I could easily prove'
  ('Now don't!' said the angry Lisette),
'The lady is always in love —
  In love with herself — the Coquette!

'There — do not be angry — you know,
  My dear little Cousin Lisette,
You told me a moment ago
  To paint *you* — a thorough Coquette!'

JOHN GODFREY SAXE

JUSTINE, YOU LOVE ME NOT

I KNOW, Justine, you speak me fair
  As often as we meet;
And 'tis a luxury, I swear,
  To hear a voice so sweet;
And yet it does not please me quite,
  The civil way you've got;
For me you're something too polite —
  Justine, you love me not!

I know, Justine, you never scold
  At aught that I may do:
If I am passionate or cold,
  'Tis all the same to you.
'A charming temper,' say the men,
  'To smooth a husband's lot;'
I wish 'twere ruffled now and then —
  Justine, you love me not!

I know, Justine, you wear a smile
  As beaming as the sun;
But who supposes all the while
  It shines for only one?

41

Though azure skies are fair to see,
  A transient cloudy spot
In yours would promise more to me —
  Justine, you love me not!

I know, Justine, you make my name
  Your eulogistic theme,
And say — if any chance to blame —
  You hold me in esteem.
Such words, for all their kindly scope,
  Delight me not a jot;
Just as you would have praised the Pope —
  Justine, you love me not!

I know, Justine — for I have heard
  What friendly voices tell —
You do not blush to say the word,
  'You like me passing well';
And thus the fatal sound I hear
  That seals my lonely lot:
There's nothing now to hope or fear —
  Justine, you love me not!

JOHN GODFREY SAXE

THE GROOMSMAN TO HIS MISTRESS

EVERY wedding, says the proverb,
  Makes another, soon or late;
Never yet was any marriage
  Entered in the book of Fate,

42

But the names were also written
  Of the patient pair that wait.

Blessings then upon the morning
  When my friend, with fondest look,
By the solemn rites' permission,
  To himself his mistress took,
And the Destinies recorded
  Other two within their book.

While the priest fulfilled his office,
  Still the ground the lovers eyed,
And the parents and the kinsmen
  Aimed their glances at the bride,
But the groomsmen eyed the virgins
  Who were waiting at her side.

Three there were that stood beside her;
  One was dark, and one was fair,
But nor fair nor dark the other,
  Save her Arab eyes and hair;
Neither dark nor fair I call her,
  Yet she was the fairest there.

While her groomsman — shall I own it?
  Yes, to thee, and only thee —
Gazed upon this dark-eyed maiden
  Who was fairest of the three,
Thus he thought: 'How blest the bridal
  Where the bride were such as she!'

43

Then I mused upon the adage
  Till my wisdom was perplexed,
And I wondered, as the churchman
  Dwelt upon his holy text,
Which of all who heard his lesson
  Should require the service next.

Whose will be the next occasion
  For the flowers, the feast, the wine?
Thine perchance, my dearest lady,
  Or, who knows? — it may be mine:
What if 'twere — forgive the fancy —
  What if 'twere — both mine and thine?

                    THOMAS WILLIAM PARSONS

SAINT VALENTINE'S DAY

THIS day was sacred once to Pan,
  And kept with song and wine;
But when our better creed began
  'Twas held no more divine,
Until there came a holy man,
  One Bishop Valentine.

He, finding, as all good men will,
  Much in the ancient way
That was not altogether ill,
  Restored the genial day,
And we the pagan fashion still
  With pious hearts obey.

44

Without this custom, all would go
    Amiss in Love's affairs,
All passion would be poor dumb show,
    Pent sighs and secret prayers;
And bashful maids would never know
    What timid swain was theirs.

Ah, many things with mickle pains
    Without reward are done!
A thousand poets rack their brains
    For her who loves but one;
Yea, many weary with their strains
    The nymph that cares for none!

Yet, should no faithful heart be faint
    To give affection's sign:
So, dearest, let mine own acquaint
    With its emotions — thine;
And blessings on that fine old Saint,
    Good Bishop Valentine!

THOMAS WILLIAM PARSONS

A MUSICAL BOX

I KNOW her, the thing of laces, and silk,
    And ribbons, and gauzes, and crinoline,
With her neck and shoulders as white as milk,
    And her doll-like face and conscious mien.
A lay-figure fashioned to fit a dress,
    All stuffed within with straw and bran;

Is that a woman to love, to caress?
Is that a creature to charm a man?

Only listen! how charmingly she talks
    Of your dress and hers — of the Paris mode —
Of the coming ball — of the opera box —
    Of jupons, and flounces, and fashions abroad.
Not a bonnet in church but she knows it well,
    And Fashion she worships with downcast eyes;
A *marchande de modes* is her oracle,
    And Paris her earthly paradise.

She's perfect to whirl with in a waltz;
    And her shoulders show well on a soft divan,
As she lounges at night and spreads her silks,
    And plays with her bracelets and flirts her fan;
With a little laugh at whatever you say,
    And rounding her 'No' with a look of surprise:
And lisping her 'Yes,' with an air distrait,
    And a pair of aimless, wandering eyes.

Her duty this Christian never omits!
    She makes her calls, and she leaves her cards,
And enchants a circle of half-fledged wits,
    And slim attachés and six-foot Guards.
Her talk is of people, who're nasty or nice,
    And she likes little bon-bons of compliments;
While she seasons their sweetness by way of spice,
    By some witless scandal she often invents.

46

Is this the thing for a mother or wife?
   Could love ever grow on such barren rocks?
Is this a companion to take for life?
   One might as well marry a musical box!
You exhaust in a day her full extent;
   'Tis the same little tinkle of tunes always;
You must wind her up with a compliment,
   To be bored with the only airs she plays.

WILLIAM WETMORE STORY

SNOWDROP

WHEN, full of warm and eager love,
   I clasp you in my fond embrace,
You gently push me back and say,
   'Take care, my dear, you'll spoil my lace!'

You kiss me just as you would kiss
   Some woman friend you chanced to see;
You call me 'dearest.' — All love's forms
   Are yours, not its reality.

Oh, Annie! cry, and storm, and rave!
   Do anything with passion in it!
Hate me an hour, and then turn round
   And love me truly, just one minute.

WILLIAM WETMORE STORY

47

WITHOUT AND WITHIN

My coachman, in the moonlight there,
  Looks through the side-light of the door;
I hear him with his brethren swear,
  As I could do, — but only more.

Flattening his nose against the pane,
  He envies me my brilliant lot,
Breathes on his aching fists in vain,
  And dooms me to a place more hot.

He sees me in to supper go,
  A silken wonder by my side,
Bare arms, bare shoulders, and a row
  Of flounces, for the door too wide.

He thinks how happy is my arm
  'Neath its white-gloved and jeweled load;
And wishes me some dreadful harm,
  Hearing the merry corks explode.

Meanwhile I inly curse the bore
  Of hunting still the same old coon,
And envy him, outside the door,
  In golden quiets of the moon.

The winter wind is not so cold
  As the bright smile he sees me win,
Nor the host's oldest wine so old
  As our poor gabble sour and thin.

I envy him the ungyved prance
  By which his freezing feet he warms,
And drag my lady's chains and dance
  The galley-slave of dreary forms.

O, could he have my share of din,
  And I his quiet! — past a doubt
'Twould still be one man bored within,
  And just another bored without.

JAMES RUSSELL LOWELL

AUF WIEDERSEHEN

The little gate was reached at last,
  Half hid in lilacs down the lane;
She pushed it wide, and, as she passed,
A wistful look she backward cast,
  And said, — '*Auf wiedersehen!*'

With hand on latch, a vision white
  Lingered reluctant, and again
Half doubting if she did aright,
Soft as the dews that fell at night,
  She said, — '*Auf wiedersehen!*'

The lamp's clear gleam flits up the stair;
  I linger in delicious pain;
Ah, in that chamber, whose rich air
To breathe in thought I scarcely dare,
  Thinks she, — '*Auf wiedersehen?*'

'Tis thirteen years; once more I press
  The turf that silences the lane;
I hear the rustle of her dress,
I smell the lilacs, and — ah, yes,
  I hear, — '*Auf wiedersehen!*'

Sweet piece of bashful maiden art!
  The English words had seemed too fain,
But these — they drew us heart to heart,
Yet held us tenderly apart;
  She said, — '*Auf wiedersehen!*'

JAMES RUSSELL LOWELL

THE PETITION

OH, tell me less or tell me more,
Soft eyes with mystery at the core,
That always seem to meet my own
Frankly as pansies fully blown,
Yet waver still 'tween no and yes!

So swift to cavil and deny,
Then parley with concessions shy,
Dear eyes, that share their youth with mine
And through my inmost shadows shine,
Oh, tell me more or tell me less!

JAMES RUSSELL LOWELL

THE PROTEST

I COULD not bear to see those eyes
On all with wasteful largess shine,
And that delight of welcome rise
Like sunshine strained through amber wine,
But that a glow from deeper skies,
From conscious fountains more divine,
Is (is it?) mine.

Be beautiful to all mankind,
As Nature fashioned thee to be;
'Twould anger me did all not find
The sweet perfection that's in thee;
Yet keep one charm of charms behind, —
Nay, thou'rt so rich, keep two or three
For (is it?) me!

JAMES RUSSELL LOWELL

THE LAWYER'S INVOCATION TO SPRING

WHEREAS, on certain boughs and sprays
  Now divers birds are heard to sing,
And sundry flowers their heads upraise,
  Hail to the coming on of Spring!

The songs of those said birds arouse
  The memory of our youthful hours,
As green as those said sprays and boughs,
  As fresh and sweet as those said flowers.

The birds aforesaid — happy pairs —
  Love, 'mid the aforesaid boughs, inshrines
In freehold nests; themselves their heirs,
  Administrators, and assigns.

O busiest term of Cupid's Court,
  Where tender plaintiffs action bring, —
Season of frolic and of sport,
  Hail, as aforesaid, coming Spring!

HENRY HOWARD BROWNELL

MAKE BELIEVE

Kiss me, though you make believe,
  Kiss me, though I almost know
You are kissing to deceive;
  Let the tide one moment flow
Backward ere it rise and break,
Only for poor pity's sake!

Give me of your flowers one leaf,
  Give me of your smiles one smile,
Backward roll the tide of grief
  Just a moment, though, the while,
I should feel and almost know
You are trifling with my woe.

Whisper to me sweet and low;
  Tell me how you sit and weave

Dreams about me, though I know
    It is only make believe!
Just a moment, though 'tis plain
You are jesting with my pain.

ALICE CARY

THERE'S A TIME TO BE JOLLY

THERE'S a time to be jolly, a time to repent,
A season for folly, a season for Lent,
The first as the worst we too often regard;
The rest as the best, but our judgment is hard.

There are snows in December and roses in June,
There's darkness at midnight and sunshine at noon;
But, were there no sorrow, no storm-cloud or rain,
Who'd care for the morrow with beauty again.

The world is a picture both gloomy and bright,
And grief is the shadow and pleasure the light,
And neither should smother the general tone;
For where were the other if either were gone?

The valley is lovely; the mountain is drear,
Its summit is hidden in mist all the year;
But gaze from the heaven, high over all weather,
And mountain and valley are lovely together.

I have learned to love Lucy, though faded she be;
If my next love be lovely, the better for me.

By the end of next summer, I'll give you my oath,
It was best, after all, to have flirted with both.

CHARLES GODFREY LELAND

NOTHING TO WEAR

MISS FLORA McFLIMSEY, of Madison Square,
Has made three separate journeys to Paris;
And her father assures me, each time she was there,
That she and her friend Mrs. Harris
(Not the lady whose name is so famous in history
But plain Mrs. H., without romance or mystery)
Spent six consecutive weeks without stopping,
In one continuous round of shopping: —
Shopping alone, and shopping together,
At all hours of the day, and in all sorts of weather:
For all manner of things that a woman can put
On the crown of her head or the sole of her foot,
Or wrap round her shoulders, or fit round her waist,
Or that can be sewed on, or pinned on, or laced,
Or tied on with a string, or stitched on with a bow,
In front or behind, above or below;
For bonnets, mantillas, capes, collars, and shawls;
Dresses for breakfasts, and dinners, and balls;
Dresses to sit in, and stand in, and walk in,
Dresses to dance in, and flirt in, and talk in;
Dresses in which to do nothing at all;
Dresses for winter, spring, summer, and fall, —
All of them different in color and pattern,
Silk, muslin, and lace, crape, velvet and satin,

Brocade, and broadcloth, and other material
Quite as expensive and much more ethereal:
In short, for all things that could ever be thought of,
Or milliner, modiste, or tradesman be bought of,
From ten-thousand-francs robes to twenty-sous frills;
In all quarters of Paris, and to every store:
While McFlimsey in vain stormed, scolded, and swore.
They footed the streets, and he footed the bills.

The last trip, their goods shipped by the steamer *Argo*
Formed, McFlimsey declares, the bulk of her cargo,
Not to mention a quantity kept from the rest,
Sufficient to fill the largest-sized chest,
Which did not appear on the ship's manifest,
But for which the ladies themselves manifested
Such particular interest that they invested
Their own proper persons in layers and rows
Of muslins, embroideries, worked underclothes,
Gloves, handkerchiefs, scarfs, and such trifles as those;
Then, wrapped in great shawls, like Circassian beauties,
Gave *good-by* to the ship, and *go-by* to the duties.
Her relations at home all marvelled, no doubt,
That Flora had grown so enormously stout
For an actual belle and a possible bride;
But the miracle ceased when she turned inside out,
And the truth came to light, and the dry-goods beside,
Which, in spite of collector and custom-house sentry,
Had entered the port without any entry.
And yet, though scarce three months have passed since
the day

The merchandise went, on twelve carts, up Broadway,
The same Miss McFlimsey, of Madison Square,
The last time we met, was in utter despair,
Because she had nothing whatever to wear!

Nothing to wear! Now, as this is a true ditty,
I do not assert — this you know is between us —
That she's in a state of absolute nudity,
Like Power's Greek Slave, or the Medici Venus;
But I do mean to say I have heard her declare,
When at the moment she had on a dress
Which cost five hundred dollars, and not a cent less,
And jewelry worth ten times more, I should guess,
That she had not a thing in the wide world to wear!
I should mention just here, that out of Miss Flora's
Two hundred and fifty or sixty adorers,
I had just been selected as he who should throw all
The rest in the shade, by the gracious bestowal
On myself, after twenty or thirty rejections
Of those fossil remains which she called her 'affections,'
And that rather decayed but well-known work of art
Which Miss Flora persisted in styling 'her heart.'
So we were engaged. Our troth had been plighted
Not by moonbeam or starbeam, by fountain or grove,
But in a front parlor, most brilliantly lighted,
Beneath the gas-fixture we whispered our love —
Without any romance, or raptures, or sighs,
Without any tears in Miss Flora's blue eyes,
Or blushes, or transports, or such silly actions;
It was one of the quietest business transactions,

With a very small sprinkling of sentiment, if any,
And a very large diamond imported by Tiffany.
On her virginal lips while I printed a kiss,
She exclaimed, as sort of a parenthesis,
And by way of putting me quite at my ease,
'You know I'm to polka as much as I please,
And flirt when I like, — now stop, — don't you speak, —
And you must not come here more than twice in a week,
Or talk to me either at party or ball;
But always be ready to come when I call:
So don't prose to me about duty and stuff, —
If we don't break this off, there will be time enough
For that sort of thing; but the bargain must be,
That as long as I choose I am perfectly free:
For this is a sort of engagement, you see,
Which is binding on you, but not binding on me.'

Well, having thus wooed Miss McFlimsey, and gained
        her,
With the silks, crinolines, and hoops that contained her,
I had, as I thought, a contingent remainder
At least in the property, and the best right
To appear as its escort by day and by night;
And it being the week of the Stuckups' grand ball, —
Their cards had been out for a fortnight or so,
And set all the Avenue on the tiptoe, —
I considered it only my duty to call
And see if Miss Flora intended to go.
I found her as ladies are apt to be found
When the time intervening between the first sound

Of the bell and the visitor's entry is shorter
Than usual — I found — I won't say I caught — her
Intent on the pier-glass, undoubtedly meaning
To see if perhaps it didn't need cleaning.
She turned as I entered — 'Why, Harry, you sinner,
I thought that you went to the Flashers' to dinner!'
'So I did,' I replied, 'but the dinner is swallowed,
And digested, I trust; for 'tis now nine or more:
So being relieved from that duty, I followed
Inclination, which led me, you see, to your door.
And now will your Ladyship so condescend
As just to inform me if you don't intend
Your beauty and graces and presence to lend
(All of which, when I own, I hope no one will borrow)
To the Stuckups, whose party, you know, is tomorrow?'
The fair Flora looked up with a pitiful air,
And answered quite promptly, 'Why, Harry, *mon cher*,
I should like above all things to go with you there,
But really and truly — I've nothing to wear.'

'Nothing to wear? Go just as you are:
Wear the dress you have on, and you'll be by far,
I engage, the most bright and particular star
On the Stuckup horizon — ' I stopped, for her eye,
Notwithstanding this delicate onset of flattery,
Opened on me at once a most terrible battery
Of scorn and amazement. She made no reply,
But gave a slight turn to the end of her nose
(That pure Grecian feature), as much as to say,
'How absurd that any sane man should suppose

That a lady would go to a ball in the clothes,
No matter how fine, that she wears every day!'
So I ventured again — 'Wear your crimson brocade.'
(Second turn-up of nose) — 'That's too dark by a
    shade.' —
'Your blue silk —' 'That's too heavy.' — 'Your
    pink —' 'That's too light.' —
'Wear tulle over satin.' — 'I can't endure white.' —
'Your rose-colored, then, the best of the batch.' —
'I haven't a thread of point-lace to match.' —
'Your brown moire-antique' — 'Yes, and look like a
    Quaker.' —
'The pearl-colored —' 'I would, but that plaguey
    dress-maker
Has had it a week.' — 'Then that exquisite lilac,
In which you would melt the heart of a Shylock.'
(Here the nose took again the same elevation) —
'I wouldn't wear that for the whole of creation.' —
'Why not? It's my fancy, there's nothing could strike it
As more *comme il faut.*' — 'Yes, but, dear me, that
    lean
Sophronia Stuckup has got one just like it,
And I won't appear dressed like a chit of sixteen.' —
'Then that splendid purple, that sweet mazarine,
That superb point D'aiguille, that imperial green,
That zephyr-like tarlatan, that rich grenadine.' —
'Not one of all which is fit to be seen,'
Said the lady, becoming excited and flushed.
'Then wear,' I exclaimed, in a tone which quite crushed
Opposition, 'that gorgeous toilette which you sported

In Paris last spring at the grand presentation,
When you quite turned the head of the head of the
      nation;
And by all the grand court were so very much courted.
The end of the nose was portentously tipped up,
And both the bright eyes shot forth indignation,
As she burst upon me with the fierce exclamation,
'I have worn it three times at the least calculation,
And that and most of my dresses are ripped up!'
Here I ripped out something, perhaps rather rash —
Quite innocent, though; but to use an expression
More striking than classic, it 'settled my hash,'
And proved very soon the last act of our session.
'Fiddlesticks, is it, sir? I wonder the ceiling
Doesn't fall down and crush you! Oh, you men have no
      feeling!
You selfish, unnatural, illiberal creatures,
Who set yourselves up as patterns and preachers,
Your silly pretence — why, what a mere guess it is!
Pray, what do you know of a woman's necessities?
I have told you and shown you I've nothing to wear,
And it's perfectly plain you not only don't care,
But you do not believe me' — (here the nose went still
      higher):
'I suppose if you dared you would call me a liar.
Our engagement is ended, sir — yes, on the spot;
You're a brute and a monster, and — I don't know
      what.'
I mildly suggested the words Hottentot,
Pickpocket, and cannibal, Tartar, and thief,

As gentle expletives which might give relief;
But this only proved as a spark to the powder,
And the storm I had raised came faster and louder;
It blew and it rained, thundered, lightened, and hailed
Interjections, verbs, pronouns, till language quite failed
To express the abusive, and then its arrears
Were brought up all at once by a torrent of tears;
And my last faint, despairing attempt at an obs-
Ervation was lost in a tempest of sobs.

Well, I felt for the lady, and felt for my hat too,
Improvised on the crown of the latter a tattoo,
In lieu of expressing the feelings which lay
Quite too deep for words, as Wordsworth would say:
Then, without going through the form of a bow,
Found myself in the entry, — I hardly knew how, —
On doorstep and sidewalk, past lamp-post and square,
At home and up-stairs, in my own easy-chair;
Poked my feet into slippers, my fire into blaze,
And said to myself, as I lit my cigar, —
Supposing a man had the wealth of the Czar
Of the Russias to boot, for the rest of his days,
On the whole do you think he would have much time to
     spare
If he married a woman with nothing to wear?

WILLIAM ALLEN BUTLER

WHEN LOVELY WOMAN

When lovely woman wants a favor,
  And finds, too late, that man won't bend,
What earthly circumstance can save her
  From disappointment in the end?

The only way to bring him over,
  The last experiment to try,
Whether a husband or a lover,
  If he have feeling is — to cry.

PHŒBE CARY

UNDER THE ROSE

She wears a rose in her hair
  At the twilight's dreamy close:
Her face is fair, *how* fair
  Under the rose!

I steal like a shadow there
  As she sits in rapt repose,
And whisper my loving prayer
  Under the rose!

She takes the rose from her hair,
  And her color comes and goes,
And I — a lover will dare
  Under the rose!

RICHARD HENRY STODDARD

PROUD LOVER

I NEVER yet could understand
   How men could love in vain;
I hold it weak and wrong to love
   And not be loved again.
For me, I must have heart for heart,
Deny me that, and we must part.

There be who love, or think they love,
   Without return for years;
They waste their days in fruitless sighs,
   Their nights in hopeless tears.
Not such am I: my heart is free,
I love not her who loves not me!

               RICHARD HENRY STODDARD

PROPOSAL

THE violet loves a sunny bank,
   The cowslip loves the lea,
The scarlet creeper loves the elm,
   But I love — thee.

The sunshine kisses mount and vale,
   The stars they kiss the sea,
The west winds kiss the clover bloom,
   But I kiss — thee.

The oriole weds his mottled mate,
   The lily's bride o' the bee;

Heaven's marriage ring is round the earth, —
Shall I wed thee?

BAYARD TAYLOR

BATTLEDORES

MAY is blond and Madge is brown,
   And 'twixt the two I fly;
One lives in country, one in town,
   But yet for both I sigh.
Madge says that I'm in love with May,
   And pouts a sweet disdain,
Yet all the while her brown eyes say
   'I fear no rival's reign.'

May is calm, and like the moon
   That sails the summer sky,
Her voice is sweeter than the tune
   The scented night-winds sigh;
And underneath her quiet glance
   All happily I lie,
And live a dreamy, sweet romance
   When her fair form is nigh.

Thus 'twixt the two my heart is thrown,
   And shuttle-like I fly;
For blue-eyed May is all my own
   When brown Madge is not by.
But loving each, and loving both,
   I know not how to lie,

So here's to both, however loth,
　Good-by! — good-by! — good-by!

FITZ JAMES O'BRIEN

SERENADE

HIDE, happy damask, from the stars,
　What sleep enfolds behind your veil,
But open to the fairy cars
　On which the dreams of midnight sail;
And let the zephyrs rise and fall
　About her in the curtained gloom,
And then return to tell me all
　The silken secrets of the room.

Ah, dearest, may the elves that sway
　Thy fancies come from emerald plots,
Where they have dozed and dreamed all day
　In hearts of blue forget-me-nots!
And one perhaps shall whisper thus:
　Awake! and light the darkness, Sweet!
While thou art reveling with us,
　He watches in the lonely street.

HENRY TIMROD

FEMININE ARITHMETIC

Laura

On me he shall ne'er put a ring,
  So, mamma, 'tis in vain to take trouble —
For I was but eighteen in spring,
  While his age exactly is double.

Mamma

He's but in his thirty-sixth year,
  Tall, handsome, good-natured and witty,
And should you refuse him, my dear,
  May you die an old maid without pity!

Laura

His figure, I grant you, will pass,
  And at present he's young enough plenty;
But when I am sixty, alas!
  Will not he be a hundred and twenty?

CHARLES GRAHAM HALPINE

WIDOW-OLOGY

Oh, none of your boarding-school misses,
  Your sweet, timid creatures for me —
Who rave about Cupid and blisses,
  Yet know not what either may be!
I don't feel at all sentimental,
  Nor care I for Byron a rap,

But give me a jolly and gentle
  Young widow in weeds and a cap!

To her I would offer my duty,
  For, in truth, all belief it exceeds
To find how the blossom of beauty
  Is heightened by peeping from 'weeds.'
She is armed *cap-a-pie* for the struggle;
  To her cap I a captive belong,
And the wink of her magical ogle
  Is a challenge to courtship and song.

The tremors of girlhood are over;
  Love's blossom has ripened to fruit;
And her first love asleep under clover
  Is the soil where my passion takes root.
'Tis pleasant to know the departed
  Was tenderly cared to the last —
And that she will not die broken-hearted
  If I should pop off just as fast.

Her temper is never so restive,
  Her duty she knows, and a shape
Is never so sweetly suggestive
  As when it is muffled in crape.
The maid wears one ring when she marries,
  In proof she all others discards,
But the widow-wife wiselier carries
  A pair of these marital guards.

So none of your boarding-school misses,
  Your sweet, timid creatures for me,
Who rave about Cupid and blisses,
  Yet know not what either may be!
I don't feel at all sentimental,
  Nor care I for Byron a rap,
Give me a plump, jolly and gentle
  Young widow in weeds and a cap!

CHARLES GRAHAM HALPINE

TWO TRUTHS

'DARLING,' he said, 'I never meant
  To hurt you.' And his eyes were wet.
'I would not hurt you for the world:
  Am I to blame if I forget?'

'Forgive my selfish tears!' she cried,
  'Forgive! I knew that it was not
Because you meant to hurt me, sweet, —
  I knew it was that you forgot!'

But all the same, deep in her heart
  Rankled this thought, and rankles yet:
When love is at its best one loves
  So much that he cannot forget.

HELEN HUNT JACKSON

TOUJOURS AMOUR

PRITHEE tell me, Dimple-Chin,
At what age does Love begin?
Your blue eyes have scarcely seen
Summers three, my fairy queen,
But a miracle of sweets,
Soft approaches, sly retreats,
Show the little archer there,
Hidden in your pretty hair;
When didst learn a heart to win?
Prithee tell me, Dimple-Chin!

'Oh!' the rosy lips reply,
'I can't tell you if I try.
'Tis so long I can't remember:
Ask some younger lass than I!'

Tell, O tell me, Grizzled-Face,
Do your heart and head keep pace?
When does hoary Love expire,
When do frosts put out the fire?
Can its embers burn below
All that chill December snow?
Care you still soft hands to press,
Bonny heads to smooth and bless?
When does Love give up the chase?
Tell, O tell me, Grizzled-Face!

'Ah!' the wise old lips reply,
'Youth may pass and strength may die;

'But of Love I can't foretoken:
Ask some older sage than I!'
EDMUND CLARENCE STEDMAN

WITCHCRAFT

OUR great-great-grandpapas had schooled
   Your fancies, Lita, were you born
In days when Cotton Mather ruled
   And damask petticoats were worn!
Your pretty ways, your mocking air,
   Had passed, mayhap, for Satan's wiles —
As fraught with danger, then and there,
   To you, as now to us your smiles.

Why not? Were inquest to begin,
   The tokens are not far to seek:
Item — the dimple of your chin;
   Item — that freckle on your cheek.
Grace shield his simple soul from harm
   Who enters yon flirtation niche,
Or trusts in whispered counter-charm,
   Alone with such a parlous witch!

Your fan a wand is, in disguise;
   It conjures, and we straight are drawn
Within a witches' Paradise
   Of music, germans, roses, lawn.
So through the season, where you go,
   All else than Lita men forget:

70

One needs no second-sight to know
  That sorcery is rampant yet.

Now, since the bars no more await
  Fair maids that practice sable arts,
Take heed, while I pronounce the fate
  Of her who thus ensnares men's hearts:
In time you shall a wizard meet
  With spells more potent than your own,
And you shall know your master, Sweet,
  And for these witcheries atone.

For you at his behest shall wear
  A veil, and seek with him the church,
And at the altar rail forswear
  The craft that left you in the lurch;
But oft thereafter, musing long,
  With smile, and sigh, and conscience-twitch,
You shall too late confess the wrong —
  A captive and repentant witch.

EDMUND CLARENCE STEDMAN

THE DOORSTEP

THE conference-meeting through at last,
  We boys around the vestry waited
To see the girls come tripping past
  Like snow-birds willing to be mated.

Not braver he that leaps the wall
  By level-musket flashes litten,

Than I, that stepped before them all
     Who longed to see me get the mitten.

But no, she blushed and took my arm!
     We let the old folks have the highway,
And started toward the Maple Farm
     Along a kind of lovers' by-way.

I can't remember what we said,
     'Twas nothing worth a song or story;
Yet that rude path by which we sped
     Seemed all transformed and in a glory.

The snow was crisp beneath our feet,
     The moon was full, the fields were gleaming;
By hood and tippet sheltered sweet,
     Her face with youth and health was beaming.

The little hand outside her muff, —
     O sculptor, if you could but mould it! —
So lightly touched my jacket-cuff,
     To keep it warm I had to hold it.

To have her with me there alone, —
     'Twas love and fear and triumph blended.
At last we reached the foot-worn stone
     Where that delicious journey ended.

The old folks, too, were almost home;
     Her dimpled hand the latches fingered,

72

We heard the voices nearer come,
  Yet on the doorstep still we lingered.

She shook her ringlets from her hood
  And with a 'Thank you, Ned,' dissembled,
And yet I knew she understood
  With what a daring wish I trembled.

A cloud passed kindly overhead,
  The moon was slyly peeping through it,
Yet hid its face, as if it said,
  'Come, now or never! do it! *do it!*'

My lips till then had only known
  The kiss of mother and of sister,
But somehow, full upon her own
  Sweet, rosy, darling mouth, — I kissed her!

Perhaps 'twas boyish love, yet still,
  O listless woman, weary lover!
To feel once more that fresh, wild thrill
  I'd give — but who can live youth over.

                    EDMUND CLARENCE STEDMAN

THE WORLD WELL LOST

THAT year? Yes, doubtless I remember still, —
  Though why take count of every wind that blows!
'Twas plain, men said, that Fortune used me ill
  That year, — the selfsame year I met with Rose.

Crops failed; wealth took a flight; house, treasure,
    land,
  Slipped from my hold — thus plenty comes and goes.
One friend I had, but he too loosed his hand
  (Or was it I?) the year I met with Rose.

There was a war, I think; some rumor, too,
  Of famine, pestilence, fire, deluge, snows;
Things went awry. My rivals, straight in view,
  Throve, spite of all; but I, — I met with Rose.

That year my white-faced Alma pined and died:
  Some trouble vexed her quiet heart, — who knows?
Not I, who scarcely missed her from my side,
  Or aught else gone, the year I met with Rose.

Was there no more? Yes, that year life began:
  All life before a dream, false joys, light woes, —
All after-life compressed within the span
  Of that one year, — the year I met with Rose.

EDMUND CLARENCE STEDMAN

THE GOLDEN FISH

Love is a little golden fish,
  Wondrous shy... ah, wondrous shy...
You may catch him if you wish;
He might make a dainty dish...
  But I...
  Ah, I've other fish to fry!

For when I try to snare this prize,
   Earnestly and patiently,
All my skill the rogue defies,
Lurking safe in Aimée's eyes...
      So, you see,
      I am caught and Love goes free!

GEORGE ARNOLD

WHAT SHE SAID ABOUT IT

LYRICS to Inez and Jane,
   Dolores and Ethel and May;
Señoritas distant as Spain,
   And damsels just over the way!

It is not that I'm jealous, not that,
   Of either Dolores or Jane,
Of some girl in an opposite flat,
   Or in one of his castles in Spain,

But it is that salable prose
   Put aside for this profitless strain,
I sit the day darning his hose —
   And he sings of Dolores and Jane.

Though the winged-horse must caracole free —
   With the pretty, when 'spurning the plain,'
Should the team-work fall wholly on me
   While he soars with Dolores and Jane?

75

I am neither Dolores nor Jane,
　But to lighten a little my life
Might the Poet not spare me a strain —
　Although I am only his wife!

CHARLES HENRY WEBB

THE KING AND THE POPE

THE King and the Pope together
Have written a letter to me;
It is signed with a golden sceptre,
It is sealed with a golden key.
The King wants me out of his eyesight;
The Pope wants me out of his See.

The King and the Pope together
Have a hundred acres of land:
I do not own the foot of ground
On which my two feet stand;
But the prettiest girl in the kingdom
Strolls with me on the sand.

The King has a hundred yeomen
Who will fight for him any day,
The Pope has priests and bishops
Who for his soul will pray:
I have only one little sweetheart
But she'll kiss me when I say.

The King is served at his table
By ladies of high degree;

The Pope has never a true love,
So a cardinal pours his tea:
No ladies stand round me in waiting,
But my sweetheart sits by me.

And the King with his golden sceptre,
And the Pope with Saint Peter's key,
Can never unlock the one little heart
That is opened only to me.
For I am the Lord of a Realm,
And I am Pope of a See;
Indeed, I'm supreme in the kingdom
That is sitting just now on my knee!

CHARLES HENRY WEBB

DICTUM SAPIENTI

THAT 'tis well to be off with the old love
    Before one is on with the new
Has somehow passed into a proverb, —
    But I never have found it true.

No love can be quite like the old love,
    Whate'er may be said for the new —
And if you dismiss me, my darling,
    You may come to this thinking, too.

Were the proverb not wiser if mended,
    And the fickle and wavering told

77

To be sure they're on with the new love
Before they are off with the old?
CHARLES HENRY WEBB

EVANESCENCE

WHAT's the brightness of a brow?
  What's a mouth of pearls and corals?
Beauty vanishes like a vapor,
  Preach the men of musty morals!

Should the crowd then, ages since,
  Have shut their ears to singing Homer,
Because the music fled as soon
  As fleets the violets' aroma?

Ah, for me, I thrill to see
  The bloom a velvet cheek discloses.
Made of dust? — I well believe it!
  So are lilies, so are roses!
HARRIET PRESCOTT SPOFFORD

A SIGH

IT was nothing but a rose I gave her, —
  Nothing but a rose
Any wind might rob of half its savor,
  Any wind that blows.

When she took it from my trembling fingers
  With a hand as chill, —

Ah, the flying touch upon them lingers,
  Stays, and thrills them still!

Withered, faded, pressed between the pages,
  Crumpled fold on fold, —
Once it lay upon her breast, and ages
  Cannot make it old!

HARRIET PRESCOTT SPOFFORD

FRENCH WITH A MASTER

TEACH you French? I will, my dear!
Sit and con your lesson here.
What did Adam say to Eve?
Aimer, aimer; c'est à vivre.

Don't pronounce the last word long;
Make it short to suit the song;
Rhyme it to your flowing sleeve,
Aimer, aimer; c'est à vivre.

Sleeve, I said, but what's the harm
If I really meant your arm?
Mine shall twine it (by your leave),
Aimer, aimer; c'est à vivre.

Learning French is full of slips;
Do as I do with the lips;
Here's the right way, you perceive,
Aimer, aimer; c'est à vivre.

French is always spoken best
Breathing deeply from the chest;
Darling, does your bosom heave?
Aimer, aimer; c'est à vivre.

Now, my dainty little sprite,
Have I taught your lesson right?
Then what pay shall I receive?
Aimer, aimer; c'est à vivre.

Will you think me overbold
If I linger to be told
Whether you yourself believe
Aimer, aimer; c'est à vivre.

Pretty pupil, when you say
All this French to me today,
Do you mean it, or deceive?
Aimer, aimer; c'est à vivre.

Tell me, may I understand,
When I press your little hand,
That our hearts together cleave?
Aimer, aimer; c'est à vivre.

Have you in your tresses room
For some orange-buds to bloom?
May I such a garland weave?
Aimer, aimer; c'est à vivre.

Or, if I presume too much
Teaching French by sense of touch,
Grant me pardon and reprieve!
Aimer, aimer; c'est à vivre.

Sweetheart, no! you cannot go!
Let me sit and hold you so;
Adam did the same to Eve, —
Aimer, aimer; c'est à vivre.

THEODORE TILTON

NO AND YES

I WATCHED her at her spinning,
And this was my beginning
Of wooing and of winning.

So cruel, so uncaring,
So scornful was her bearing,
She set me half despairing.

Yet sorry wit one uses,
Who loves, and thinks he loses
Because a maid refuses.

Love prospers in the making
By help of all its aching,
And quaking, and heart-breaking.

A woman's first denying
Betokens her complying
Upon a second trying.

81

When first I said in pleading,
'Behold, my love lies bleeding! —'
She shook her head unheeding.

But when again I told her,
And blamed her growing colder,
She dropped against my shoulder.

Then with her eyes of splendor,
She gave a look so tender,
I knew she would surrender!

So down the lane I led her,
And while her cheek grew redder,
I sued outright to wed her.

Good end from bad beginning!
My wooing came to winning! —
And still I watch her spinning!

THEODORE TILTON

THE WITCH IN THE GLASS

'My mother says I must not pass
Too near that glass;
She is afraid that I will see
A little witch that looks like me,
With a red, red mouth to whisper low
The very thing I should not know!'

82

'Alack, for all your mother's care!
A bird of the air,
A wistful wind, or (I suppose
Sent by some hapless boy) a rose,
With breath too sweet, will whisper low
The very thing you should not know!'

SARAH M. B. PIATT

NOCTURNE

Up to her chamber window
A slight wire trellis goes,
And up this Romeo's ladder
Clambers a bold white rose.

I lounge in the ilex shadows,
I see the lady lean,
Unclasping her silken girdle,
The curtain's folds between.

She smiles on her white-rose lover,
She reaches out her hand
And helps him in at the window —
I see it where I stand!

To her scarlet lip she holds him,
And kisses him many a time —
Ah, me! it was he that won her
Because he dared to climb!

THOMAS BAILEY ALDRICH

L'EAU DORMANTE

CURLED up and sitting on her feet,
  Within the window's deep embrasure,
Is Lydia; and across the street,
  A lad, with eyes of roguish azure,
Watches her buried in her book.
In vain he tries to win a look,
And from the trellis over there
Blows sundry kisses through the air,
Which miss the mark, and fall unseen,
Uncared for. Lydia is thirteen.

My lad, if you, without abuse,
  Will take advice from one who's wiser,
And put his wisdom to more use
  Than ever yet did your adviser;
If you will let, as none will do,
Another's heartbreak serve for two,
You'll have a care, some four years hence,
How you lounge there by yonder fence
And blow those kisses through that screen —
For Lydia will be seventeen.

THOMAS BAILEY ALDRICH

ON AN ITAGLIO HEAD OF MINERVA

BENEATH the warrior's helm, behold
  The flowing tresses of the woman!
Minerva, Pallas, what you will —
  A winsome creature, Greek or Roman.

Minerva? No! 'tis some sly minx
  In cousin's helmet masquerading;
If not — then Wisdom was a dame
  For sonnets and for serenading!

I thought the goddess cold, austere,
  Not made for love's despairs and blisses:
Did Pallas wear her hair like that?
  Was Wisdom's mouth so shaped for kisses?

The Nightingale should be her bird,
  And not the Owl, big-eyed and solemn:
How very fresh she looks, and yet
  She's older far than Trajan's column!

The magic hand that carved this face,
  And set this vine-work round it running,
Perhaps ere mighty Phidias wrought
  Had lost its subtle skill and cunning.

Who was he? Was he glad or sad,
  Who knew to carve in such a fashion?
Perchance he graved the dainty head
  For some brown girl that scorned his passion.

Perchance, in some still garden-place,
  Where neither fount nor tree today is,
He flung the jewel at the feet
  Of Phryne, or perhaps 'twas Laïs.

But he is dust; we may not know
  His happy or unhappy story:
Nameless, and dead these centuries,
  His work outlives him — there's his glory!

Both man and jewel lay in earth
  Beneath a lava-buried city;
The countless summers came and went
  With neither haste, nor hate, nor pity.

Years blotted out the man, but left
  The jewel fresh as any blossom,
Till some Visconti dug it up —
  To rise and fall on Mabel's bosom!

O nameless brother! see how Time
  Your gracious handiwork has guarded:
See how your loving, patient art
  Has come, at last, to be rewarded.

Who would not suffer slights of men,
  And pangs of hopeless passion also,
To have his carven agate-stone
  On such a bosom rise and fall so!

THOMAS BAILEY ALDRICH

PALABRAS CARIÑOSAS

GOOD-NIGHT! I have to say good-night
To such a host of peerless things!
Good-night unto the fragile hand
All queenly with its weight of rings;
Good-night to fond, uplifted eyes,
Good-night to chestnut braids of hair,
Good-night unto the perfect mouth,
And all the sweetness nestled there —
   The snowy hand detains me, then
   I'll have to say Good-night again!

But there will come a time, my love,
When, if I read our stars aright,
I shall not linger by this porch
With my adieus. Till then, good-night!
You wish the time were now? And I.
You do not blush to wish it so?
You would have blushed yourself to death
To own so much a year ago —
   What, both those snowy hands! ah, then
   I'll have to say Good-night again!

THOMAS BAILEY ALDRICH

COMEDY

THEY parted, with clasps of hand,
And kisses, and burning tears.
They met, in a foreign land,
After some twenty years:

Met as acquaintances meet,
Smilingly, tranquil-eyed —
Not even the least little beat
Of the heart, upon either side!

They chatted of this and that,
The nothings that make up life;
She in a Gainsborough hat,
And he in black for his wife.

Ah, what a comedy this!
Neither was hurt, it appears:
Yet once she had leaned to his kiss,
And once he had known her tears!

THOMAS BAILEY ALDRICH

CAPRICE

SHE hung the cage at the window:
　'If he goes by,' she said,
'He will hear my robin singing,
　And when he lifts his head,
I shall be sitting here to sew,
And he will bow to me, I know.'

The robin sang a love-sweet song,
  The young man raised his head;
The maiden turned away and blushed;
  'I am a fool!' she said,
And went on broidering in silk
A pink-eyed rabbit, white as milk.

The young man loitered slowly
  By the house three times that day;
She took her bird from the window:
  'He need not look this way.'
She sat at her piano long,
And sighed, and played a death-sad song.

But when the day was done, she said,
  'I wish that he would come!
Remember, Mary, if he calls
  Tonight — I'm not at home!'
So when he rang, she went — the elf! —
She went and let him in herself.

WILLIAM DEAN HOWELLS

THE WHITE FLAG

I SENT my love two roses, — one
  As white as driven snow,
And one a blushing royal red,
  A flaming Jacqueminot.

I meant to touch and test my fate;
  That night I should divine,

The moment I should see my love,
   If her true heart were mine.

For if she holds me dear, I said,
   She'll wear my blushing rose;
If not, she'll wear my cold Lamarque,
   As white as winter's snows.

My heart sank when I met her: sure
   I had been overbold,
For on her breast my pale rose lay
   In virgin whiteness cold.

Yet with low words she greeted me,
   With smiles divinely tender;
Upon her cheek the red rose dawned, —
   The white rose meant surrender.

JOHN HAY

HER LETTER

I'M sitting alone by the fire,
   Dressed just as I came from the dance,
In a robe even *you* would admire, —
   It cost a cool thousand in France;
I'm be-diamonded out of all reason,
   My hair is done up in a cue:
In short, sir, 'the belle of the season'
   Is wasting an hour on you.

A dozen engagements I've broken;
   I left in the midst of a set;
Likewise a proposal, half spoken,
   That waits — on the stairs — for me yet.
They say he'll be rich, — when he grows up, —
   And then he adores me indeed.
And you, sir, are turning your nose up,
   Three thousand miles off as you read.

'And how do I like my position?'
   'And what do I think of New York?'
'And now, in my higher ambition,
   With whom do I waltz, flirt, or talk?'
'And isn't it nice to have riches,
   And diamonds and silks, and all that?'
'And aren't they a change to the ditches
   And tunnels of Poverty Flat?'

Well, yes, — if you saw us out driving
   Each day in the park, four-in-hand, —
If you saw poor dear mamma contriving
   To look supernaturally grand, —
If you saw papa's picture, as taken
   By Brady, and tinted at that, —
You'd never suspect he sold bacon
   And flour at Poverty Flat.

And yet, just this moment, when sitting
   In the glare of the grand chandelier, —
In the bustle and glitter befitting

The 'finest *soirée* of the year, —'
In the mists of a *gauze de Chambéry*,
  And the hum of the smallest of talk, —
Somehow, Joe, I thought of the 'Ferry,'
  And the dance that we had on 'The Fork';

Of Harrison's barn, with its muster
  Of flags festooned over the wall;
Of the candles that shed their soft lustre
  And tallow on head-dress and shawl;
Of the steps that we took to one fiddle;
  Of the dress of my queer *vis-à-vis*;
And how I once went down the middle
  With the man that shot Sandy McGee;

Of the moon that was quietly sleeping
  On the hill when the time came to go;
Of the few baby peaks that were peeping
  From under their bed-clothes of snow;
Of that ride, — that to me was the rarest;
  Of — the something you said at the gate, —
Ah, Joe, then I wasn't an heiress
  To 'the best-paying lead in the State.'

Well, well, it's all past; yet it's funny
  To think, as I stood in the glare
Of fashion and beauty and money,
  That I should be thinking, right there,
Of some one who breasted high water,
  And swam the North Fork, and all that,

Just to dance with old Folinsbee's daughter,
  The Lily of Poverty Flat.

But goodness! what nonsense I'm writing!
  (Mamma says my taste still is low,)
Instead of my triumphs reciting
  I'm spooning on Joseph, — heigh-ho!
And I'm to be 'finished' by travel, —
  Whatever's the meaning of that, —
Oh! why did papa strike pay gravel
  In drifting on Poverty Flat?

Good night, — here's the end of my paper;
  Good night, — if the longitude please, —
For may be, while wasting my taper,
  Your sun's climbing over the trees.
But know, if you haven't got riches,
  And are poor, dearest Joe, and all that,
That my heart's somewhere there in the ditches,
  And you've struck it, — on Poverty Flat.

BRET HARTE

THE MORAL

THE play is ended? Be it so!
  What use to criticise?
And yet perhaps 'twere well to know
  What moral underlies.

For, as I read it, it is such
  As both may ponder o'er;

Had I not loved you quite so much
You might have loved me more.

ROBERT KELLEY WEEKS

UNDERSONG

While I linger in her room,
Sitting idly at her feet,
Si douce est la Marguerite,
Are the clover blossoms sweet?
Are the apple-trees in bloom,
While I linger in her room?

Is there murmuring of bees
While I murmur at her feet,
Si douce est la Marguerite?
Is there singing swift and sweet
By the brook-side, in the trees?
Is there murmuring of bees?

In the springtime of the year,
Sitting singing at her feet,
Si douce est la Marguerite,
Is there then no other sweet
Thing to see or have or hear
In the springtime of the year?

ROBERT KELLEY WEEKS

EVE'S DAUGHTER

I WAITED in the little sunny room:
  The cool breeze waved the window-lace, at play,
The white rose on the porch was all in bloom,
  And out upon the bay
I watched the wheeling sea-birds go and come.

'Such an old friend, — she would not make me stay
  While she bound up her hair.' I turned, and lo,
Danaë in her shower! and fit to slay
  All a man's hoarded prudence at a blow:
Gold hair that streamed away
  As round some nymph a sunlit fountain's flow.
  'She would not make me wait!' — but well I know
She took a good half-hour to loose and lay
  Those locks in dazzling disarrangement so!

EDWARD ROWLAND SILL

TO A MAID DEMURE

OFTEN when the night is come,
With its quiet group at home,
While they broider, knit, or sew,
Read, or chat in voices low,
Suddenly you lift your eyes
With an earnest look, and wise;
But I cannot read their lore, —
Tell me less, or tell me more.

Like a picture in a book,
Pure and peaceful is your look,
Quietly you walk your ways;
Steadfast duty fills the days.
Neither tears nor fierce delights,
Feverish days nor tossing nights,
Any troublous dreams confess, —
Tell me more, or tell me less.

Swift the weeks are on the wing;
Years are brief, and love a thing
Blooming, fading, like a flower;
Wake and seize the little hour.
Give me welcome or farewell;
Quick! I wait! And who can tell
What tomorrow may befall, —
Love me more, or not at all.

EDWARD ROWLAND SILL

APPRECIATED

'Ah, could I but be understood!'
    (I prayed the powers above)
'Could but some spirit, bright and good,
    Know me and, knowing, love!'

One summer's day there came to pass —
    A maid; and it befell
She spied and knew me; yea, alas!
    She knew me all too well.

96

Gray were the eyes of Rosamund,
  And I could see them see
Through and through me, and beyond,
  And care no more for me.

                    EDWARD ROWLAND SILL

THE LOVER'S SONG

LEND me thy fillet, Love!
  I would no longer see;
Cover mine eyelids close awhile,
  And make me blind like thee.

Then might I pass her sunny face,
  And know not it was fair;
Then might I hear her voice, nor guess
  Her starry eyes were there.

Ah! banished so from stars and sun —
  Why need it be my fate?
If only she might dream me good
  And wise, and be my mate!

Lend her thy fillet, Love!
  Let her no longer see:
If there is hope for me at all,
  She must be blind like thee.

                    EDWARD ROWLAND SILL

THE LOVE-KNOT

Tying her bonnet under her chin,
She tied her raven ringlets in;
But not alone in the silken snare
Did she catch her lovely floating hair,
For, tying her bonnet under her chin,
She tied a young man's heart within.

They were strolling together up the hill,
Where the wind comes blowing merry and chill;
And it blew the curls, a frolicsome race,
All over the happy peach-colored face,
Till, scolding and laughing, she tied them in,
Under her beautiful dimpled chin.

And it blew a color, bright as the bloom
Of the pinkest fuchsia's tossing plume,
All over the cheeks of the prettiest girl
That ever imprisoned a romping curl,
Or, tying her bonnet under her chin,
Tied a young man's heart within.

Steeper and steeper grew the hill;
Madder, merrier, chillier still
The western wind blew down, and played
The wildest tricks with the little maid,
As, tying her bonnet under her chin,
She tied a young man's heart within.

O western wind, do you think it was fair
To play such tricks with her floating hair?

To gladly, gleefully do your best
To blow her against the young man's breast,
Where he as gladly folded her in,
And kissed her mouth and her dimpled chin?

Ah! Ellery Vane, you little thought,
An hour ago, when you besought
This country lass to walk with you,
After the sun had dried the dew,
What perilous danger you'd be in,
As she tied her bonnet under her chin!

NORA PERRY

YESTERDAY

WHAT if but yesterday
I laughed and said him nay,
When here's today, today
To change my mind and say
A sweeter word than nay.

What if but yesterday
I told him that my nay
Could never turn to yea,
Though he should pray and pray
Forever and a day.

What if but yesterday
He swore he would obey
My cruel will, nor stay

To further sue or pray, —
Then strode in wrath away.

What if but yesterday
Like this he strode away,
When here's today, today —
For him to hear me say, —
'I love you, Love, today!'

NORA PERRY

EVENING SONG

Look off, dear love, across the sallow sands,
    And mark yon meeting of the sun and sea,
How long they kiss in sight of all the lands.
    Ah! longer, longer, we.

Now in the sea's red vintage melts the sun,
    As Egypt's pearl dissolved in rosy wine,
And Cleopatra night drinks all. 'Tis done,
    Love, lay thine hand in mine.

Come forth, sweet stars, and comfort heaven's heart;
    Glimmer, ye waves, round else unlighted sands.
O night! divorce our sun and sky apart,
    Never our lips, our hands.

SIDNEY LANIER

SONG

Not from the whole wide world I chose thee —
 Sweetheart, light of the land and the sea!
The wide, wide world could not inclose thee,
 For thou art the whole wide world to me.

RICHARD WATSON GILDER

WHITE, PILLARED NECK

White, pillared neck; a brow to make men quake;
 A woman's perfect form;
Like some cool marble, should that wake,
 Breathe, and be warm.

A shape, a mind, a heart
 Of womanhood the whole;
Her breath, her smile, her touch, her art,
 All — save her soul.

RICHARD WATSON GILDER

WHY

Why need a pretty woman chat
 When, from her sweet shut lips,
A language well worth looking at
 In silent utterance slips?

Why need a clever woman speak
 Her wit or wisdom, for

Each man she meets, — dull, mild or meek, —
  Feels her superior?

Why need an ugly — No! — I fall
  Back to one simple cry —
Why, why need woman speak at all?...
  There is no reason why!
                    MADELINE BRIDGES
                    (MARY AINGE DE VERE)

THE WHOLE STORY

THEY met and bowed and moved apart —
  They met and danced, and yet
Again they met, and talked and walked —
  And afterward, they met,
And met, and met, and met — and then
They met — and did not part again!
                    MADELINE BRIDGES
                    (MARY AINGE DE VERE)

HER MILKING PAIL

WHEN Doris took her milking pail
  To cross the dewy meadow,
The eastern sky was golden pale,
  The valley lay in shadow;
I followed slowly, not too near,
And softly, lest the maid should hear.

102

The wet white daisies bent to touch
   Her slender foot, and kiss it;
I envied them this pleasure much,
   Since I'd been doomed to miss it;
And thought the flowers were treated **far**
More kindly than some lovers are.

Behind a thorn I stood to watch
   Her coax the cow, and chide her,
And humming at a merry catch,
   Set the small stool beside her;
While freshly as she could have wished
The milk through dimpled fingers swished.

Thought I: 'this chance I must not miss!
   Her milk pail I will carry;
And in.return demand a kiss;
   For milkmaids are not chary,
The poets sing, if swains be brave;
Hence my reward I'll boldly crave.'

But when at length I would have stept
   Toward the maid with fervor,
Young Strephon o'er the hedge had leapt
   With like intent to serve her;
And lest his chance might later fail,
Took first — a kiss! and then — the pail!

Unseen I sought a shaded path,
   And left the lovers cooing;

But now my verse a moral hath:...
   Whatever's worth the doing
You'll find — each day the story tells —
Is being done by some one else!

MADELINE BRIDGES

(MARY AINGE DE VERE)

DROPPING CORN

PRETTY Phœbe Lane and I,
   In the soft May weather,
Barefoot down the furrows went
   Dropping corn together.

Side by side across the field
   Back and forth we hurried;
All the golden grains we dropped
   Soon the ploughshare buried.

Bluebirds on the hedges sat,
   Chirping low and billing;
'Why,' thought I, 'not follow suit,
   If the maid is willing!'

So I whispered, 'Phœbe, dear,
   Kiss me —' 'Keep on dropping!'
Called her father from the plough;
   'There's no time for stopping!'

The cord was loosed — the moment sped;
   The golden charm was broken!

Nevermore between us two
    Word of love was spoken.

What a little slip, sometimes,
    All our hope releases!
How the merest breath of chance
    Breaks our joy in pieces!

Sorrow's cup, though often drained,
    Never lacks for filling;
And we can't get Fortune's kiss
    When the maid is willing!

                    MAURICE THOMPSON

A WHITE ROSE

THE red rose whispers of passion,
    And the white rose breathes of love;
Oh, the red rose is a falcon,
    And the white rose is a dove!

But I send you a cream-white rosebud
    With a flush on its petal tips;
For the love that is purest and sweetest
    Has a kiss of desire on the lips.

                    JOHN BOYLE O'REILLY

AN EXPLANATION

HER lips were so near
  That — what else could I do?
You'll be angry, I fear,
But her lips were so near —
Well, I can't make it clear,
  Or explain it to you,
But — her lips were so near
  That — what else could I do?

WALTER LEARNED

TIME'S REVENGE

WHEN I was ten and she fifteen —
  Ah, me, how fair I thought her!
She treated with disdainful mien
  The homage that I brought her.
And, in a patronizing way,
Would of my shy advances say:
'It's really quite absurd, you see;
He's very much too young for me.'

I'm twenty now, she twenty-five —
  Well, well, how old she's growing!
I fancy that my suit might thrive
  If pressed again; but, owing
To great discrepancy in age,
Her marked attentions don't engage

My young affections, for, you see,
She's really quite too old for me.

WALTER LEARNED

ON A FLY-LEAF OF A BOOK OF OLD
PLAYS

At Cato's Head in Russel Street
   These leaves she sat a-stitching;
I fancy she was trim and neat,
   Blue-eyed and quite bewitching.

Before her on the street below,
   All powder, ruffs and laces,
There strutted idle London beaux
   To ogle pretty faces;

While, filling many a Sedan chair
   With monstrous hoop and feather,
In paint and powder London's fair
   Went trooping past together.

Swift, Addison and Pope, mayhap,
   They sauntered slowly past her,
Or printer's boy, with gown and cap,
   For Steele, went trotting faster.

For beau nor wit had she a look;
   Nor lord nor lady minding,

She bent her head above this book,
   Attentive to her binding.

And one stray thread of golden hair,
   Caught in her nimble fingers,
Was stitched within this volume where
   Until today it lingers.

Past and forgotten, beaux and fair,
   Wigs, powder, all outdated;
A queer antique, the Sedan chair,
   Pope, stiff and antiquated.

Yet as I turn these odd, old plays,
   This single stray lock finding,
I'm back in those forgotten days
   And watch her at her binding.

WALTER LEARNED

THE OLD BEAU

How cracked and poor his laughter rings!
   How dulled his eye once flashing warm!
But still a courtly pathos clings
   About his bent and withered form.

Tonight, where mirth with music dwells,
   His wrinkled cheek, his locks of snow,
Gleam near the grandsons of the belles
   He smiled on forty years ago.

We watch him here, and half believe
  Our gaze may witness, while he prates,
Death, like a footman, touch his sleeve
  And tell him that the carriage waits.

EDGAR FAWCETT

THE SCHOLAR'S SWEETHEART

ALL day he toils, with zeal severe,
  On something learnedly polemic;
From Harvard he returned last year,
  With bounteous honors academic.
His parents name him but to praise,
  His little sisters quite adore him,
And all the loving household lays
  Allegiance willingly before him!

What forms his labor, week by week?
  They could not understand — oh, never!
'Tis something eminently Greek,
  'Tis something intricately clever!
But still his task, unfinished yet,
  He shapes with industry unflagging,
And writes his treatise that shall set
  The heads of noted pundits wagging!

Is it of Homer's doubtful lines,
  Or yet some question, subtly finer?
Or whether certain famous wines
  Were first obtained from Asia Minor?

Is it of dialects impure?
  Is it some long-fought rule of grammar?
Is it old Sanscrit roots obscure?
  Is it that wearisome digamma?

But whether this or whether that,
  Through fragrant fields, when work is ended,
While darkly wheels the zigzag bat
  And all the west is warmly splendid,
He steals to meet, in loving wise,
  With eager steps that do not tarry,
A rosy girl whose shining eyes
  Grow tender as she calls him 'Harry.'

What altered thoughts can she awake,
  This pearl of sweethearts, best and fairest!
And what a contrast does she make
  To 'Comments on the Second Aorist!'
So strongly round him can she throw
  Her dazzling spells of sweet retention,
'Tis doubtful now if he could go
  Correctly through his first declension!

For while near mossy meadow-bars,
  With spirit thrilled by sacred pleasures,
He lingers till the dawn of stars,
  He lingers by the girl he treasures,
This grave young scholar scarcely knows
  If Hector was a fighting seaman,

If lofty Pindar wrote in prose,
    Or Athens lay in Lacedæmon!

ON REREADING TÉLÉMAQUE

'Calypso could not console herself'
I PLACE thee back upon the shelf,
    O Fénelon, how scant thy knowledge,
Who seemed as Solomon himself
    To me, a callow youth at college!

No need to say thou wert a priest;
    No need to own that I am human;
Mine this advantage is — at least
    I've learned the alphabet of Woman.

And yet but half the truth is told:
    I do thee wrong, sagacious Mentor, —
Calypso could not be consoled
    Until another man was sent her!

                    JAMES JEFFREY ROCHE

IF

Oh, if the world were mine, Love,
    I'd give the world for thee!
Alas, there is no sign, Love,
    Of that contingency!

III

Were I a king — which isn't
   To be considered now, —
A diadem had glistened
   Upon thy lovely brow.

Had Fame with laurels crowned me, —
   She hasn't up to date, —
Nor time nor change had found me
   To love and thee ingrate.

If Death threw down his gage, Love,
   Though Life is dear to me,
I'd die e'en of old age, Love,
   To win a smile from thee.

But being poor we part, Dear,
   And love, sweet love, must die, —
Thou wilt not break thy heart, Dear,
   No more, I think, shall I.

JAMES JEFFREY ROCHE

BIFTEK AUX CHAMPIGNONS

MIMI, do you remember —
   Don't get behind your fan —
That morning in September
   On the cliffs of Grand Manan;
Where to the shock of Fundy
   The topmost harebells sway
(*Campanula rotundi-*
   folia: cf. Gray)?

On the pastures high and level,
　That overlook the sea,
Where I wondered what the devil
　Those little things could be
That Mimi stooped to gather,
　As she strolled across the down,
And held her dress skirt rather —
　Oh, now, you needn't frown!

For you know the dew was heavy,
　And your boots, *I* know, were thin:
So a little extra brevi-
　ty in skirts was, sure, no sin.
Besides, who minds a cousin?
　First, second, even third —
I've kissed 'em by the dozen,
　And they never once demurred.

'If one's allowed to ask it,'
　Quoth I, '*ma belle cousine*,
What have you in your basket?'
　(Those baskets white and green
The brave Passamaquoddies
　Weave out of scented grass,
And sell to tourist bodies
　Who through Mount Desert pass.)

You answered, slightly frowning,
　'Put down your stupid book —
That everlasting Browning —
　And come and help me look.

Mushroom you spik him English,
   I call him *champignon*:
I'll teach you to distinguish
   The right kind from the wrong.'

There was no fog on Fundy
   That blue September day;
The west wind, for that one day,
   Had swept it all away.
The lighthouse glasses twinkled,
   The white gulls screamed and flew,
The merry sheep bells tinkled,
   The merry breezes blew.

The bayberry aromatic
   The papery immortelles ,
(That give our grandma's attic
   That sentimental smell,
Tied up in little brush-brooms)
   Were sweet as new-mown hay,
While we went hunting mushrooms
   That blue September day.

In each small juicy dimple
   Where turf grew short and thick,
And nibbling teeth of simple
   Sheep had browsed it to the quick;
Where roots or bits of rotten
   Wood were strewed, we found a few
Young buttons just begotten
   Of morning sun and dew.

And you compared the shiny,
　　Soft, creamy skin, that hid
The gills so pink and tiny,
　　To your gloves of undressed kid,
While I averred the color
　　Of the gills, within their sheath,
Was like — but only duller —
　　The rosy palms beneath.

As thus we wandered, sporting
　　In idleness of mind,
There came a fearful snorting
　　And trampling close behind;
And, with a sudden plunge, I
　　Upset the basketful
Of those accursed fungi,
　　As you shrieked, 'The bull!　The bull!'

And then we clung together
　　And faced the enemy,
Which proved to be a wether
　　And scared much worse than we.
But while that startled mutton
　　Went scampering away,
The mushrooms — every button —
　　Had tumbled in the bay.

The basket had a cover,
　　The wind was blowing stiff,
And rolled that basket over

The edges of the cliff.
It bounced from crag to boulder;
  It leaped and whirled in air,
But while you clutched my shoulder
  I did not greatly care.

I tried to look as rueful
  As though each mushroom there
Had been a priceless truffle,
  But yet I did not care.
And ever since that Sunday
  On the cliffs of Grand Manan,
High over the surf of Fundy
  I've used the kind they can.

HENRY AUSTIN BEERS

THOUGHTS ON THE COMMANDMENTS

'LOVE your neighbor as yourself,' —
  So the parson preaches:
That's one half the Decalogue, —
  So the prayer-book teaches.
Half my duty I can do
  With but little labor,
For with all my heart and soul
  I do love my neighbor.

Mighty little credit, that,
  To my self-denial:
Not to love, though, that might be
  Something of a trial.

Why, the rosy light that peeps
  Through the glass above her
Lingers round her lips, — you see
  E'en the sunbeams love her.

So, to make my merit more,
  I'll go beyond the letter: —
Love my neighbor as myself?
  Yes, and ten times better.
For she's sweeter than the breath
  Of the Spring, that passes
Through the fragrant, budding woods,
  O'er the meadow grasses.

And I've preached the word I know,
  For it was my duty
To convert the stubborn heart
  Of the little beauty.
Once again success has crowned
  Missionary labor,
For her sweet eyes own that she
  Also loves her neighbor.

GEORGE A. BAKER

'LE DERNIER JOUR D'UN CONDAMNÉ'

Old coat, for some three or four seasons
  We've been jolly comrades, but now
We part, old companion, forever;
  To fate and to fashion I bow.

117

You'd look well enough at a dinner,
 I'd wear you with pride at a ball;
But I'm dressing tonight for a wedding —
 My own — and you'd not do at all.

You've too many wine-stains about you,
 You're scented too much with cigars,
When the gas-light shines full on your collar
 It glitters on myriad stars
That wouldn't look well at my wedding;
 They'd seem inappropriate there —
Nell doesn't use diamond powder,
 She tells me it ruins her hair.

You've been out on Cozzen's piazza
 Too late, when the evenings were damp,
When the moonbeams were silvering Cro'nest,
 And the lights were all out in the camp.
You've rested on highly-oiled stairways
 Too often, when sweet eyes were bright,
And somebody's ball dress — not Nellie's —
 Flowed round you in rivers of white.

There's a reprobate looseness about you;
 Should I wear you tonight, I believe,
As I come with my bride from the altar
 You'd laugh in your wicked old sleeve,
When you felt there the tremulous pressure
 Of her hand, in its delicate glove,
That is telling me shyly, but proudly,
 Her trust is as deep as her love.

So, go to your grave in the wardrobe,
    And furnish a feast for the moth,
Nell's love shall betray its sweet secrets
    To younger, more innocent cloth.
'Tis time to put on your successor —
    It's made in a fashion that's new;
Old coat, I'm afraid it will never
    Sit as easily on me as you.

                    GEORGE A. BAKER

TO MISTRESS PYRRHA

WHAT perfumed, posie-dizened sirrah,
    With smiles for diet,
Clasps you, O fair but faithless Pyrrha,
    On the quiet?
For whom do you bind up your tresses,
    As spun-gold yellow, —
Meshes that go with your caresses
    To snare a fellow?

How will he rail at fate capricious,
    And curse you duly,
Yet now he deems your wiles delicious, —
    You perfect, truly!
Pyrrha, your love's a treacherous ocean;
    He'll soon fall in there!
Then shall I gloat on his commotion,
    For I have been there!

                    EUGENE FIELD

LOVER'S LANE, SAINT JO

Saint Jo, Buchanan County,
  Is leagues and leagues away;
And I sit in the gloom of this rented room
  And pine to be there today.
Yes, with London fog around me
  And the bustling to and fro,
I am fretting to be across the sea
  In Lover's Lane, Saint Jo.

I would have a brown-eyed maiden
  Go driving once again;
And I'd sing the song, as we snailed along,
  That I sung to that maiden then:
I purposely say, 'as we *snailed* along,'
  For a proper horse goes slow
In those leafy aisles, where Cupid smiles,
  In Lover's Lane, Saint Jo.

From her boudoir in the alders
  Would peep a lynx-eyed thrush,
And we'd hear her say, in a furtive way,
  To the noisy cricket, 'Hush!'
To think that the curious creature
  Should crane her neck to know
The various things one says and sings
  In Lover's Lane, Saint Jo!

But the maples they should shield us
  From the gossips of the place;

Nor should the sun, except by pun,
  Profane the maiden's face;
And the girl should do the driving,
  For a fellow can't, you know,
Unless he's neglectful of what's quite respectful
  In Lover's Lane, Saint Jo.

Ah! sweet the hours of springtime,
  When the heart inclines to woo,
And it's deemed all right for the callow wight
  To do what he wants to do;
But cruel the age of winter
  When the way of the world says no
To the hoary men who would woo again
  In Lover's Lane, Saint Jo!

In the Union Bank of London
  Are forty pounds or more,
Which I'm like to spend, ere the month shall end,
  In an antiquarian store;
But I'd give it all, and gladly,
  If for an hour or so
I could feel the grace of a distant place, —
  Of Lover's Lane, Saint Jo.

EUGENE FIELD

A ROSE

'Twas a Jacqueminot rose
    That she gave me at parting;
Sweetest flower that blows.
'Twas a Jacqueminot rose.
In the lone garden-close,
    With the swift blushes starting,
'Twas a Jacqueminot rose
    That she gave me at parting.

If she kissed it, who knows —
    Since I will not discover,
And lone is that close —
If she kissed it, who knows?
Or if not the red rose,
    Perhaps then the lover!
If she kissed it, who knows,
    Since I will not discover?

Yet at least with the rose
    Went a kiss that I'm wearing!
More I will not disclose;
Yet at least with the rose
Went *whose* kiss no one knows,
    Since I'm only declaring
That at least with the rose
    Went a kiss that I'm wearing.

ARLO BATES

THE SUNSHINE OF THINE EYES

THE sunshine of thine eyes,
    (O still, celestial beam!)
Whatever it touches it fills
    With the life of its lambent gleam.

The sunshine of thine eyes,
    O let it fall on me!
Though I be but a mote of the air
    I could turn to gold for thee!

GEORGE PARSONS LATHROP

THE GAME OF CHESS

'TWAS stinging, blustering winter weather;
    How well I recollect the night
When Kate and I played chess together!
    Her beauty in the hearthfire's light
Seemed more Madonna-like and rosy;
The hours were swift, the room was cosy,
    The windows frosted, silvery white.

Even now I see that grave face resting
    Upon the hand, so white and small;
I see that mystic grace, suggesting
    A painter's dream, and I recall
Her glance, now anxious, gay, or tender;
The girlish form, complete yet slender,
    In silhouette against the wall.

123

It was not strange that I was mated,
  For 'twas my fondly cherished aim.
I longed to speak, but I was fated,
  The rightful opening never came.
I pawned my heart for her sweet favor,
With every look some vantage gave her,
  And so, alas, I lost the game!

Since then by fortune, love, forsaken,
  Through checkered years I've passed and seen
My castles fall, my pawns all taken,
  My spotless knights prove traitors mean;
And worn, with many a check, I wander
Like the poor vanquished king, and ponder
  With sadness on my long-lost queen.

                              DAVID SKAATS FOSTER

I JOURNEYED SOUTH TO MEET THE SPRING

I JOURNEYED south to meet the Spring
  To feel the soft tide's gentle rise
That to my heart again should bring,
Foretold by many a whispering wing,
  The old, the new, the sweet surprise.

For once, the wonder was not new —
  And yet it wore a newer grace;
For all its innocence of hue,

Its warmth and bloom and dream and dew,
    I had but left — in Helen's face.

ROBERT UNDERWOOD JOHNSON

LOVE IN THE CALENDAR

WHEN chinks in April's windy dome
    Let through a day of June,
And foot and thought incline to roam,
    And every sound's a tune;
When Nature fills a fuller cup,
    And hides with green the gray, —
Then, lover, pluck your courage up
    And try your fate in May.

Though proud she was as sunset clad
    In Autumn's fruity shades,
Love too is proud, and brings (gay lad!)
    Humility to maids.
Scorn not from Nature's mood to learn,
    Take counsel of the day:
Since haughty skies to tender turn,
    Go try your fate in May.

Though cold she seemed as pearly light
    Adown December eves,
And stern as night when March winds smite
    The beech's lingering leaves;
Yet love hath seasons like the year,
    And grave will turn to gay, —

Then, lover, hearken not to fear,
    But try your fate in May.

And you whose art it is to hide
    The constant love you feel,
Beware, lest overmuch of pride
    Your happiness shall steal.
No longer pout, for May is here,
    And hearts will have their way;
Love's in the calendar, my dear,
    So yield to fate — and May!

ROBERT UNDERWOOD JOHNSON

BALLADE OF THE ENGAGED YOUNG MAN

Oh, I am engaged to be married now,
    And fondly dream of the happy day
When orange blossoms shall deck her brow;
    She's fixed the date for the month of May.
    And yet to myself I softly say,
As her holiday presents go ding-a-ling
    On the jeweler's flashing crystal tray,
'I wish I had put it off till spring!'

As a prince I am merry, all allow;
    I'm like a bird in the hawthorn spray,
Or a clam when the tide is high, I vow,
    Or a child with his latest toy at play.
    Yet I have to think, as I coolly lay

126

My earnings down to hear Patti sing,
    'Though my lady's an angel in every way,
I wish I had put it off till spring!'

I dance and I romp and I wonder how
    I should ever be happy or blithe or gay,
Did not Love with his sweets my heart endow —
    (He endowed when she said she'd be mine for aye)
    Yet when roses I get, or the bright coupé,
And down to the charity ball we wing,
    I fancy of sense I have not a ray,
And wish I had put it off till spring!

ENVOY

Young man, I am neither old nor gray;
    But I can inform you of just one thing:
You'll chant, if you get her December 'Yea,'
    'I wish I had put it off till spring!'

RICHARD KENDALL MUNKITTRICK

AN OLD BEAU

FULL often I think in my trim swallow-tail,
At parties where flowers their fragrance exhale,
Of times when my pate was a bower of curls,
And I danced with the grandmas of all the dear girls.

I look on the charms that their beauties unfold —
They seem the same damsels while I have grown old.

I feel like white winter without a warm ray;
They look like the roses that blossom in May.

But winter may look with its shiver and chill
Through the windows at flowers that bloom on the sill,
And I may ask Edith with ringlets of jet
If she will dance with me the next minuet.

I go to all parties, receptions, first nights,
I'm a merry old bird in my fanciful flights;
I may look like the winter a snowy old thing,
But deep in my heart dwells the spirit of spring.

I know that I am not as old as I look,
My voice has no crack and my back has no crook;
And happy I'd be if May, Maud and Lucille
Would treat me as one who's as young as I feel.

RICHARD KENDALL MUNKITTRICK

GROWING OLD

At six — I well remember when —
I fancied all folks old at ten.

But when I'd turned my first decade,
Fifteen appeared more truly staid.

But when the fifteenth round I'd run,
I thought none old till twenty one.

Then oddly, when I'd reached that age,
I held that thirty made folks sage.

But when my thirtieth year was told,
I said: 'At twoscore men grow old!'

Yet twoscore came and found me thrifty,
And so I drew the line at fifty.

But when I reached that age, I swore
None could be old until threescore!

And here I am at sixty now,
As young as when at six, I trow!

'Tis true, my hair is somewhat gray,
And that I use a cane, today;

'Tis true these rogues about my knee
Say 'Grandpa!' when they speak to me;

But, bless your soul, I'm young as when
I thought all people old at ten!

Perhaps a little wiser grown —
Perhaps some old illusions flown;

But wondering still, while years have rolled,
When is it that a man grows old?

MARC COOK

THE QUEEN OF HEARTS

MUD-STAINED and torn upon the sidewalk lying,
  Stripped of the glory of her regal parts,
Yet still the turn of fortune's wheel defying,
  I found today this tattered queen of hearts.

Where now, I wonder, are her old companions,
  The fifty one inseparable friends?
In beer saloons, or Rocky Mountain canyons —
  At sea, or in the earth's remotest ends?

Like Israel's tribe they're tossed about and scattered,
  The kings themselves perhaps have grown unclean;
And yet, though cast aside and mud-bespattered,
  The exile queen of hearts is still a queen.

Who knows but sometime jeweled fingers shuffled
  The pack in which she held an honored place?
Who knows what placid tempers she has ruffled
  At whist, by trumping an obtrusive ace?

Or when the higher honors both were boarded,
  And she was queen indeed of all the pack,
How proudly did she take the last trump hoarded,
  How, like a woman, did she win the jack!

And ah, how fondly was her face regarded
  By him who saw its deeply crimson blush,
Just after he had doubtingly discarded
  A spade, and drawn to hearts to fill a flush!

And possibly — for cards are evil's marrow,
  And queens are sometimes instruments of sin —
'Tis possible, I say, that, turned at faro,
  The queen has caused the coppered stack to win.

Her life, I fancy opened bright and merry,
  But unremittent play brought penance dear;
And so perchance from *rouge-et-noir* and sherry
  She came in time to pinochle and beer.

And then — ah, well, no sermon need I utter! —
  Enough to know she lost her winning arts,
And, all forsaken, sank into the gutter,
  Like many another luckless queen of hearts!

MARC COOK

VALENTINE

IF thou canst make the frost be gone,
  And fleet away the snow
    (And that thou canst, I trow;)
If thou canst make the spring to dawn,
Hawthorne to put her bravery on,
Willow, her weeds of fine green lawn,
  Say why thou dost not so —
    Aye, aye!
    Say why
Thou dost not so!

If thou canst chase the stormy rack,
  And bid the soft winds blow

(And that thou canst, I trow;)
If thou canst call the thrushes back
To give the groves the songs they lack,
And wake the violet in thy track,
　　Say why thou dost not so —
　　　Aye, aye!
　　Say why
Thou dost not so!

If thou canst make my winter spring,
　　With one word breathèd low
　　(And that thou canst, I know;)
If in the closure of a ring
Thou canst to me such treasure bring,
My state shall be above a king,
　　Say why thou dost not so —
　　　Aye, aye!
　　Say why
Thou dost not so!

EDITH M. THOMAS

CANDOR

October — A Wood

'I KNOW what you're going to say,' she said,
　　As she stood up looking uncommonly tall;
　　'You're going to speak of the hectic Fall,
And say you're sorry the summer's dead.
　　And no other summer was like it, you know,

And can I imagine what made it so?
Now aren't you, honestly?' 'Yes,' I said.

'I know what you're going to say,' she said;
    'You are going to ask if I forget
    That day in June when the woods were wet,
And you carried me' — here she dropped her head —
    'Over the creek; you are going to say
    Do I remember that horrid day.
Now aren't you, honestly?' 'Yes,' I said.

'I know what you're going to say,' she said;
    'You are going to say that since that time
    You have rather tended to run to rhyme,
And,' — her clear glance fell and her cheek grew red —
    'And have I noticed your tone was queer? —
    Why, everybody has seen it here! —
Now aren't you, honestly?' 'Yes,' I said.

'I know what you're going to say,' I said;
    'You're going to say you've been much annoyed,
    And I'm short of tact — you will say devoid —
And I'm clumsy and awkward, and call me Ted,
    And I bear abuse like a dear old lamb,
    And you'll have me anyway, just as I am.
Now aren't you, honestly?'
                                'Ye-es,' she said.

HENRY CUYLER BUNNER

FEMININE

SHE might have known it in the earlier Spring, —
  That all my heart with vague desire was stirred;
And, ere the Summer winds had taken wing,
  I told her; but she smiled and said no word.

The Autumn's eager hand his red gold grasped,
  And she was silent; till from skies grown drear
Fell soft one fine, first snow-flake, and she clasped
  My neck and cried, 'Love, we have lost a year!'
                        HENRY CUYLER BUNNER

A LOST CHILD

Here's a reward for who'll find Love!
  Love is a-straying
  Ever since Maying,
Hither and yon, below, above;
  All are seeking Love!

Gone astray — between the Maying
  And the gathering of the hay,
LOVE, an urchin ever playing —
  Folk are warned against his play.

How may you know him? By the quiver,
  By the bow he's wont to bear.
First on your left there comes a shiver,
  Then a twinge — the arrow's there.

134

By his eye of pansy color,
    Deep as wounds he dealeth free;
If its hue have faded duller,
    'Tis not that he weeps for me.

By the smile that curls his mouthlet;
    By the mockery of his sigh;
By his breath, a spicy South, let
    Slip his lips of roses by.

By the devil in his dimple;
    By his lies that sound so true;
By his shaft-sting, that no simple
    Ever culled will heal for you.

By his beckonings that embolden;
    By his quick withdrawings then;
By his flying hair, a golden
    Light to lure the feet of men.

By the breast wherene'er a hurt'll
    Rankle 'neath his kerchief hid —
What? you cry; *he wore a kirtle?*
    Faith! methinks the rascal did!

Here's a reward for who'll find Love!
    Love is a-straying
    Ever since Maying;
Hither and yon, below, above,
    I am seeking Love.

                    HENRY CUYLER BUNNER

135

DA CAPO

SHORT and sweet, and we've come to the end of it —
    Our poor little love lying cold.
Shall no sonnet, then, ever be penned of it?
    Nor the joys and pains of it told?
How fair was its face in the morning,
    How close its caresses at noon,
How its evening grew chill without warning
    Unpleasantly soon!

I can't say just how we began it —
    In a blush, or a smile, or a sigh;
Fate took but an instant to plan it;
    It needs but a moment to die.
Yet — remember that first conversation,
    When the flowers you had dropped at your feet
I restored. The familiar quotation
    Was — 'Sweets to the sweet.'

Oh, their delicate perfume has haunted
    My senses a whole season through.
If there *was* one soft charm that you wanted
    The violets lent it to you.
I whispered you, life was but lonely:
    A clue which you graciously took;
And your eyes learned a look for me only —
    A very nice look.

And sometimes your hand would touch *my* hand,
    With a sweetly particular touch;

You said many things in a sigh, and
  Made a look express wonderfully much.
We smiled for the mere sake of smiling,
  And laughed for no reason but fun;
Irrational joys and beguiling —
  And all that is done.

We were idle, and played for a moment
  At a game that now neither will press:
I cared not to find out what 'No' meant;
  Nor your lips to grow yielding with 'Yes.'
Love is done with and dead; if there lingers
  A faint and indefinite ghost,
It is laid with this kiss on your fingers —
  A jest at the most.

'Tis a commonplace, stale situation,
  Now the curtain comes down from above
On the end of our little flirtation —
  A travesty romance; for Love,
If he climbed in disguise to your lattice,
  Fell dead of the first kisses' pain:
But one thing is left us now; that is —
  Begin it again.

                        HENRY CUYLER BUNNER

137

ON A HYMN-BOOK

OLD hymn-book, sure I thought I'd lost you
  In the days now long gone by;
I'd forgotten where I tossed you:
  Gracious, how I sigh!

In the church a thin partition
  Stood between her pew and mine;
And her pious, sweet contrition
  Struck me as divine.

Yes, remarkably entrancing
  Was she in her sable furs;
And my eyes were always glancing
  Up, old book, to hers.

Bless you, very well she knew it,
  And I'm sure she liked it too;
Once she whispered, 'Please don't do it,'
  But her eyes said, 'Do!'

How to speak — to tell my passion?
  How to make her think me true?
Love soon found a curious fashion,
  For he spoke through you.

How I used to search your pages
  For the words I wished to say;
And received my labor's wages
  Every Sabbath day.

Ah, how sweet it was to hand her
     You, with lines I'd marked when found!
And how well I'd understand her
     When she blushed and frowned!

And one day, old book, you wriggled
     From my hand and, rattling fell
Upon the floor; and she — she giggled,
     Did Miss Isabel.

Then when next we met out walking,
     I was told in fearful tones,
How she'd got a dreadful talking
     From the Reverend Jones.

Ah, me! No man could resist her
     In those sweet and buried years,
So I think — I think I kissed her,
     Just to stop her tears.

Jones I gave a good sound chaffing;
     Called his sermon dry as bones;
Soon fair Isabel was laughing —
     Said she hated Jones.

It was after that I lost you,
     For I needed you no more;
Somewhere — anywhere I tossed you
     On a closet floor.

Reverend Samuel still preaches;
  Isabel her past atones;
In his Sunday-school she teaches —
  Mrs. Samuel Jones!

WILLIAM J. HENDERSON

CUPID AT COURT

Young Cupid strung his bow one day,
  And sallied out for sport;
As country hearts were easy prey
  Odds Darts! he went to court.

Of all that wore the puff and patch,
  Belinda led the fair:
With falbala, and fan to match,
  I trow she made him stare!

'Oho!' he cried, and quickly drew
  His bow upon the sly; —
But though he pierced her bosom through,
  She never breathed a sigh!

This was a turn, beyond a doubt,
  That filled him with amaze,
And so he sought his mother out,
  With tear-bewildered gaze.

'You silly boy,' Dame Venus said,
  'Why did you waste your art?

Go clip your curls and hide your head —
  Belinda *has* no heart!'

SAMUEL MINTURN PECK

BELINDA'S FAN

WAIF from days of puffs and patches,
  As it wafts its hint of musk,
Eerie strains of glees and catches
  Seem to echo through the dusk.
Powdered dames in satin shimmer,
  Dashing gallants gay to scan,
In the ghostly twilight glimmer
  As I wave Belinda's fan.

I can view the lustres flashing
  Down the bright assembly room;
I can hear the fountains plashing,
  I can scent the soft perfume.
Scores of eyes are blithely beaming;
  Let them beam as best they can, —
Who can match the azure-gleaming
  Eyes behind Belinda's fan?

In the courtliest of dances
  Fancy limns the fair coquette
Thrilling hearts with dimpled glances,
  Gliding through the minuet.
I can see the beaux a-flutter,
  I can read the plots they plan,

And the vows they long to utter,
　Whispering o'er Belinda's fan.

Out amid the gusty porches
　Stands Belinda's sedan chair;
Drowsy lackeys wait with torches
　For the footsteps of the fair;
And the gallants, when the revel
　Withers 'neath the morning's ban,
Wish the dawn were at the devil,
　Bowing o'er Belinda's fan.

Never owned a monarch's sceptre
　Half such power for weal or woe:
Venus' girdle never kept her
　Votaries in half the glow;
Circe's spells in magic spoken
　Weakly pale and yield the van:
Think of all the gay hearts broken —
　Broken by Belinda's fan!

SAMUEL MINTURN PECK

MY GRANDMOTHER'S TURKEY-TAIL FAN

It owned not a color that vanity dons
　Or slender wits choose for display;
Its beautiful tint was a delicate bronze,
　A brown softly blended with gray.
From her waist to her chin, spreading out without break,
　'Twas built on a generous plan:

The pride of the forest was slaughtered to make
   My grandmother's turkey-tail fan.

For common occasions it never was meant:
   In a chest between two silken cloths
'Twas kept safely hidden with careful intent
   In camphor to keep out the moths.
'Twas famed far and wide through the whole country-
      side,
   From Beersheba e'en unto Dan;
And often at meeting with envy 'twas eyed,
   My grandmother's turkey-tail fan.

Camp-meetings, indeed, were its chiefest delight.
   Like a crook unto sheep gone astray
It beckoned backsliders to re-seek the right,
   And exhorted the sinners to pray.
It always beat time when the choir went wrong,
   In psalmody leading the van.
Old Hundred, I know, was its favorite song —
   My grandmother's turkey-tail fan.

A fig for the fans that are made nowadays,
   Suited only to frivolous mirth!
A different thing was the fan that I praise,
   Yet it scorned not the good things of earth.
At bees and at quiltings 'twas aye to be seen;
   The best of the gossip began
When in at the doorway had entered serene
   My grandmother's turkey-tail fan.

Tradition relates of it wonderful tales.
   Its handle of leather was buff.
Though shorn of its glory, e'en now it exhales
   An odor of hymn-books and snuff.
Its primeval grace, if you like, you can trace:
   'Twas limned for the future to scan,
Just under a smiling gold-spectacled face,
   My grandmother's turkey-tail fan.

SAMUEL MINTURN PECK

BESSIE BROWN, M.D.

'TWAS April when she came to town;
   The birds had come, the bees were swarming.
Her name, she said, was Doctor Brown:
   I saw at once that she was charming.
She took a cottage tinted green,
   Where dewy roses loved to mingle;
And on the door, next day, was seen
   A dainty little shingle.

Her hair was like an amber wreath;
   Her hat was darker, to enhance it.
The violet eyes that glowed beneath
   Were brighter than her keenest lancet.
The beauties of her glove and gown
   The sweetest rhyme would fail to utter.
Ere she had been a day in town
   The town was in a flutter.

144

The gallants viewed her feet and hands,
    And swore they never saw such wee things;
The gossips met in purring bands
    And tore her piecemeal o'er the tea-things.
The former drank the Doctor's health
    With clinking cups, the gay carousers;
The latter watched her door by stealth,
    Just like so many mousers.

But Doctor Bessie went her way
    Unmindful of the spiteful cronies,
And drove her buggy every day
    Behind a dashing pair of ponies.
Her flower-like face so bright she bore,
    I hoped that time might never wilt her.
The way she tripped across the floor
    Was better than a philter.

Her patients thronged the village street;
    Her snowy slate was always quite full.
Some said her bitters tasted sweet;
    And some pronounced her pills delightful.
'Twas strange — I knew not what it meant —
    She seemed a nymph from Eldorado;
Where'er she came, where'er she went,
    Grief lost its gloomy shadow.

Like all the rest, I too grew ill;
    My aching heart there was no quelling.
I tremble at my doctor's bill, —
    And lo! the items still are swelling.

The drugs I've drunk you'd weep to hear!
  They've quite enriched the fair concocter,
And I'm a ruined man, I fear,
  Unless — I wed the Doctor!

SAMUEL MINTURN PECK

DUET

HE

NAY, hold me not — I must be going;
  Unwind thine arms and set me free!
The moments fly — I must be doing
  Braver deeds than kissing thee.

SHE

Have then thy will — I would not bind thee,
  Though it were death to set thee free.
Ah, me! dost think that thou wilt find thee
  A sweeter fate than kissing me?

CHARLES LOTIN HILDRETH

WHAT HE SAID

THIS kiss upon your fan I press,
  Ah, Saint Nitouche, you don't refuse it!
And may it from its soft recess,
This kiss upon your fan I press,
Be blown to you, a shy caress,
  By this white down whene'er you use it;

146

This kiss upon your fan I press,
  Ah, Saint Nitouche, you don't refuse it!

WHAT SHE THOUGHT

To kiss a fan!
  What a poky poet!
The stupid man,
To kiss a fan
When he knows that — he — can,
  Or he ought to know it.
To kiss a fan!
  What a poky poet!

HARRISON ROBERTSON

QUEL DOMMAGE

IT was just Cousin Jack, and so — what was the harm?
  We sat on the steps, for the evening was warm;
  We spoke very softly, and — as to his arm,
It was just Cousin Jack, and so — what was the harm?
  The scent of the hayfields crept up from the farm,
  We were quite in the dark, save the fireflies' swarm —
(It was just Cousin Jack, and so — what was the harm?)
  A bird, from the hedge whirring up, broke the charm;
  He bent, as I started in foolish alarm,
And — 'twas just Cousin Jack, and so — what was the
    harm?

ELEANOR PUTNAM

STOP THIEF

Love sat down like a tired tinker,
    Asking only a shady seat,
Feaster neither he was nor drinker,
    Wine nor bread would he sip nor eat.

Love slept well in the April weather —
    Laid him low where the sweet-fern grows;
Gold of gorse and the purple heather,
    Pink of poppy and rose of rose.

Love stole off in the misty dawning,
    Casting never a look behind;
Calling never a gay good morning,
    Went his way where the white ways wind.

Ye who watch for the mad marauder,
    Faring far with his gains ill got,
Stay Love's steps ere he cross the border, —
    Love has stolen — I know not what.

HERMAN KNICKERBOCKER VIELÉ

BORDERLAND

And have you been to Borderland?
Its country lies on either hand
    Beyond the river I-forget.
One crosses by a single stone
So narrow one must pass alone,

And all about its waters fret —
The laughing river I-forget.

Beneath the trees of Borderland
One seems to know and understand,
  Beside the river I-forget,
All languages of men and birds;
And all the sweet, unspoken words
  One ever missed are murmured yet
  By that sweet river I-forget.

One hears there many things afar
From cities where strange people are,
  Beyond the river I-forget;
And stranger things are in the air,
But what they are one does not care,
  For Hope lies bleeding and Regret
  Beside the river I-forget.

Some day together hand in hand
I'll take you there to Borderland,
  Beyond the river I-forget;
Some day when all our dreams come true,
One kiss for me and one for you,
  We'll watch the red sun sink and set
  Across the river I-forget.

HERMAN KNICKERBOCKER VIELÉ

149

ANNE

(Sudbury Meeting-House, 1653)

Her eyes be like the violets,
  Ablow in Sudbury lane;
When she doth smile, her face is sweet
  As blossoms after rain;
With grief I think of my gray hairs,
  And wish me young again.

In comes she through the dark old door
  Upon this Sabbath day;
And she doth bring the tender wind
  That sings in bush and tree;
And hints of all the apple boughs
  That kissed her by the way.

Our parson stands up straight and tall,
  For our dear souls to pray,
And of the place where sinners go,
  Some grewsome things doth say;
Now, she is highest Heaven to me;
  So Hell is far away.

Most stiff and still the good folk sit
  To hear the sermon through;
But if our God be such a God,
  And if these things be true,
Why did He make her then so fair,
  And both her eyes so blue?

A flickering light, the sun creeps in,
    And finds her sitting there;
And touches soft her lilac gown,
    And soft her yellow hair;
I look across to that old pew,
    And have both praise and prayer.

Oh, violets in Sudbury lane,
    Amid the grasses green,
The maid who stirs ye with her feet
    Is far more fair, I ween!
I wonder how my forty years
    Look by her sweet sixteen!

                    LIZETTE WOODWORTH REESE

ON A COLONIAL PICTURE

OUT of the dusk stepped down
    Young Beauty on the stair;
What need of April in the town
    When Dolly took the air?

Lilac the color then,
    So all in lilac she;
Her kerchief hid from maids and men
    What was too white to see.

Good Stuart folk her kin,
    And bred in Essex vales;
One looked her happy eyes within,
    And heard the nightingales.

151

When Dolly took the air,
    Each lad that happened near,
Forgetting all save she was fair,
    Turned English cavalier.

It was the end of Lent,
    The crocus lit the square;
With wavering green the bough was bent
    When Dolly took the air.

Long since that weather sped,
    Yet yonder on the wall
Her portrait holds a faded shred,
    Some scrap of it in thrall.

The New World claims the skies,
    Although the Old prevails;
We look into her happy eyes
    And hear the nightingales.

Staid lilac is her gown,
    And yellow gleams her hair;
The ghost of April is in town,
    And Dolly takes the air!

                    LIZETTE WOODWORTH REESE

A CHANGE OF FACE

IF love came up the valley
  And I went down the hill,
Do you think I'd turn and dally?
  Do you think I'd linger still?

No! no! I'd up and flout him
  And laugh his aim away:
My heart and I we'd doubt him,
  We'd doubt him night and day.

But if he'd lay his bow down
  And take a face I know,
Why, maybe, then I'd go down
  And marry with my foe.
Why, then, I'd curtsy low down
  And marry with my foe!

HARRISON SMITH MORRIS

NAKED BOUGHS

THERE were troths in the hedges
  And bird-mates were true;
There were trysts, there were pledges,
  And old loves, and new;
There was sun at the tree's heart,
  And song in the boughs,
And spring in the bee's heart,
  And whispers and vows;

There were leaves, when we mated,
  And now — naked boughs....
Ah, vows that were fated!
  Ah, loves that would house!
Your time was belated,
  Your fate — naked boughs!

HARRISON SMITH MORRIS

HELIOTROPE

AMID the chapel's chequered gloom
  She laughed with Dora and with Flora,
And chattered in the lecture-room, —
  That saucy little sophomora!
Yet while, as in her other schools,
  She was a privileged transgressor,
She never broke the simple rules
  Of one particular professor.

But when he spoke of varied lore,
  Paroxytones and modes potential,
She listened with a face that wore
  A look half fond, half reverential.
To her that earnest voice was sweet,
  And though her love had no confessor,
Her girlish heart lay at the feet
  Of that particular professor.

And he had learned, among his books
  That held the lore of ages olden,

To watch those ever changing looks,
 The wistful eyes, the tresses golden,
That stirred his pulse with passion's pain
 And thrilled his soul with soft desire,
And bade fond youth return again
 Crowned with his coronet of fire.

Her sunny smile, her winsome ways,
 Were more to him than all his knowledge,
And she preferred his words of praise
 To all the honors of the college.
Yet 'What am foolish I to him?'
 She whispered to her heart's confessor.
'She thinks me old and gray and grim,'
 In silence pondered the professor.

Yet once when Christmas bells were rung
 Above ten thousand solemn churches,
And swelling anthems grandly sung
 Pealed through the dim cathedral arches, —
Ere home returning, filled with hope,
 Softly she stole by gate and gable,
And a sweet spray of heliotrope
 Left on his littered study-table.

Nor came she more from day to day
 Like sunshine through the shadows rifting:
Above her grave, far, far away,
 The ever silent snows were drifting.

155

And those who mourned her winsome face
    Found in its stead a swift successor
And loved another in her place —
    All, save the silent old professor.

But, in the tender twilight gray,
    Shut from the sight of carping critic,
His lonely thoughts would often stray
    From Vedic verse and tongues Semitic,
Bidding the ghost of vanished hope
    Mock with its past the sad possessor
Of the dead spray of heliotrope
    That once she gave the old professor.

HARRY THURSTON PECK

MEA CULPA

THERE is a thing which in my brain,
    Though nightly I revolve it,
I cannot in the least explain,
    Nor do I hope to solve it.
While others tread the narrow path
    In manner meek and pious,
Why is it that my spirit hath
    So opposite a bias?

Brought up to fear the Lord, and dread
    The bottomless abysm,
In Watts' hymns profoundly read
    And drilled in catechism,

I should have been a model youth,
    The pink of all that's proper.
I was not, but — to tell the truth —
    I never cared a copper.

I had no yearnings when a boy
    To sport an angel's wrapper,
Nor heard I with tumultuous joy
    The church-frequenting clapper.
My actions always harmonized
    With my own sweet volition.
I always did what I devised,
    But rarely asked permission.

I went to school. To study? No!
    I dearly loved to dally
And dawdle over Ivanhoe,
    Tom Brown and Charles O'Malley:
In recitation I was used
    To halt on every sentence;
Repenting, seldom I produced
    Fruits proper to repentance.

At college, later, I became
    Familiar with my Flaccus,
Brought incense to the Muses' flame,
    And sacrificed to Bacchus.
I flourished in an air unfraught
    With sanctity's aroma;
Learned many things I was not taught,
    And captured a diploma.

I am not well provided for,
  I have no great possessions,
I do not like the legal or
  Medicinal professions;
Were I of good repute I might
  Take orders as a deacon,
But I'm no bright and shining light,
  But just a warning beacon.

Though often urged by friends sincere
  To woo some funded houri,
I cannot read my title clear
  To any damsel's dowry.
And could to wedlock I induce
  An heiress, I should falter,
For fear that such a bridal noose
  Might prove a gilded halter.

My tradesmen have suspicious grown,
  My friends are tired of giving;
Upon the cold, cold world I'm thrown
  To hammer out my living.
I fear that work before me lies —
  Indeed, I see no option,
Unless, perhaps, I advertise —
  'An orphan for adoption!'

                    EDWARD SANFORD MARTIN

SNOW–BOUND

(A law office: two briefless ones:
a clock strikes)

JAMES

ONE, two, three, four; it's four o'clock.
There comes the postman round the block,
And in a jiff we'll hear his knock
    Most pleasant.
Inform me, Thomas, will he bring
To you deserving no such thing
Letters from her whose praises ring
    Incessant?

THOMAS

Friend of my bosom, James, refrain
From putting questions fraught with pain,
And seeking facts I had not fain
    Imparted.
The said official on this stretch,
Will not, in my opinion, fetch
Such documents to me, a wretch
    Down-hearted.

JAMES

Nay; but I prithee, Thomas, tell
To me, thy friend, who loves thee well,
What cause there is for such a fell
    Deprival.
Why is it that the message fails?

Have broken ties, or twisted rails,
Or storm, or snow delayed the mail's
   Arrival?

THOMAS

Thou art, O James, a friend indeed,
To probe my wound and make it bleed;
To know of my affairs thy greed
   Hath no bound.
The reason why thou hast not guessed,
If storm there were, 'twas in her breast,
For there my letter, unexpressed,
   Lies snow-bound.

EDWARD SANFORD MARTIN

INFIRM

'I WILL not go,' he said, 'for well
I know her eyes' insidious spell,
And how unspeakably he feels
Who takes no pleasure in his meals.
I know a one-idea'd man
Should undergo the social ban,
And if she once my purpose melts
I know I'll think of nothing else.

'I care not though her teeth are pearls —
The town is full of nicer girls!
I care not though her lips are red —
It does not do to lose one's head!

I'll give her leisure to discover,
For once, how little I think of her;
And then, how will she feel?' cried he —
And took his hat and went to see.

EDWARD SANFORD MARTIN

THE CONTEMPORARY SUITOR

TIME was that Strephon when he found
   A Chloe to his mind,
Sought not how Dun reported her,
Nor lagged while Time distorted her,
But rushed right in and courted her,
   As Nature had designed.

It's different now; my Lucy, there,
   How gladly would I woo!
But shapes of such monstrosity
Confront with such ferocity
My impecuniosity —
   What is a man to do?

Strephon and Chloe had a hut,
   And though, about the door,
The wolf might raise his serenade,
No latter-day menagerie bayed
Its warning grim to man and maid:
   'Wed not if ye are poor!'

'My goats,' might Strephon say, 'will yield
   Us milk, our vineyard wine;

By olive groves my cot is hid,
No pressing wants our joy forbid,
And I can always kill a kid
  When people come to dine.'

But I, what monsters must I face
  When I for Lucy sue!
What landlords roaring for their rent!
What troops of duns by grocers sent!
And shapes of want and discontent
  Calamitous to view.

Stay, Lucy, stay! I'm bold and stout,
  I'll rout the grisly crew.
Be constant, love! and hope and wait,
And by the time you're thirty-eight
I may, perhaps, have conquered Fate,
And when I've won the right to mate,
If you're not *too* much out of date,
  I'll surely mate with you!

                    EDWARD SANFORD MARTIN

FOREWARNED

Psyche hath found her Cupid out:
And wilt thou find out me?
Then keep high heart and courage stout,
For thou'lt not see me ringed about
With Cupid's bravery.

The god's true splendor, though unguessed,
Would well illume the night;
But foolish Psyche might not rest
Till it should also bear the test
Of baser candle-light.

Thou art not Psyche, dearest maid?
Nor I the god of love.
Read, then, the riddle unafraid:
But let thy questing heart be stayed,
Nor seek her bliss to prove.

Give me the universe to roam,
The sky for breathing space,
And though my will were thistle-foam,
No breeze but yet would blow me home
To thine adored embrace.

But if thou, loving, prove the spy,
Alas! what wilt thou see?
Flaws fitted to affright the eye
In one who still hath wings to fly,
Heart-wounded, and yet — free!

ALICE BROWN

A WEST–COUNTRY LOVER

THEN, lady, at last thou art sick of my sighing.
Good-bye!
So long as I sue, thou wilt still be denying?
Good-bye!

Ah, well! shall I vow then to serve thee forever,
And swear no unkindness our kinship can sever?
Nay, nay, dear my lass! here's an end of endeavor.
Good-bye!

Yet let no sweet ruth for my misery grieve thee.
Good-bye!
The man who has loved knows as well how to leave thee.
Good-bye!
The gorse is enkindled, there's bloom on the heather,
And love is my joy, but so too is fair weather;
I still ride abroad, though we ride not together.
Good-bye!

My horse is my mate; let the wind be my master.
Good-bye!
Though Care may pursue, yet my hound follows faster.
Good-bye!
The red deer's a-tremble in coverts unbroken.
He hears the hoof-thunder; he scents the death-token.
Shall I mope at home, under vows never spoken?
Good-bye!

The brown earth's my book, and I ride forth to read it.
Good-bye!
The stream runneth fast, but my will shall outspeed it.
Good-bye!
I love thee, dear lass, but I hate the hag Sorrow.
As sun follows rain, and tonight has its morrow,

164

So I'll taste of joy, though I steal, beg, or borrow!
Good-bye!

ALICE BROWN

THE CLOVER

O RUDDY Lover —
O brave red clover!
Didst think to win her
Thou dost adore?
She will not love thee,
She looks above thee,
The Daisy's gold doth move her more.
If gold can win her,
Then Love's not in her;
So leave the sinner,
And sigh no more!

MARGARET DELAND

THE RECONCILIATION

PHYLLIS and I fell out one day,
Fell out as lovers do,
Yet why it was I could not say,
Nor do I think she knew.

Slow dragged the days down weary ways;
Birds hushed their happy cries;
Till autumn touched to sudden blaze
The world with frosty dyes.

And in a glory brief and bright
   Saint Martin's summer came,
Fringing the hills with purple light
   And the shorn fields with flame.

Then once again we met; her face,
   Her downcast, clouded eye,
Turned from me as with quickened pace
   In silence she passed by.

Upon the path her swift feet spurned,
   A tiny glove of gray
Fell with a pleading palm upturned —
   I saw it where it lay.

With wildly fluttering heart I spoke;
   Her hurrying footsteps stayed,
While on her lips a smile awoke,
   As sunshine scatters shade.

'Come, Phyllis,' said I, 'let us cease.
   An age of joy we've missed';
She said, 'Well, I have wanted peace
   This long time' — and we kissed.

Now oft, as in my wife's dear eyes
   I see fond whimsies blent,
That dropped glove stirs a vague surmise —
   Was it an accident?

JAMES BENJAMIN KENYON

166

MY MAIDEN AUNT

DEAR withered cheek — you know the hue,
Old parchment; something of a shrew,
She has not — between me and you —
    Lived much 'in clover.'
Yet seldom is she heard to sigh;
And when she smiles, from either eye
The radiating wrinkles fly
    Her face all over.

Time, laying by his scythe, I trow,
Has guided his relentless plow
Across the pallor of a brow
    Once far from homely.
And russet curls, that once she tossed
Coquettishly, are crisped with frost,
But have not altogether lost
    Their hue so comely.

I've heard — from whom I can't aver —
That fate has been unkind to her;
Old letters laid in lavender
    Reveal a lover.
But these are dated long ago,
And years have yellowed o'er their snow,
Since she, with tell-tale cheeks aglow,
    First read them over.

In escapades of day and night,
When she has risen in her might,

I've found that though her foot is light
   Her hand is heavy.
Yet, though at times she loves to pour
The vials of her anger o'er
My head, she keeps a warm spot for
   Her graceless 'nevvy.'

How oft the teasing jibe I've checked
Upon my tongue, to recollect
That she, so long denied respect,
   Does now command some!
I would not dare to even *grin*
At her, my wealthy next-of-kin,
Lest, some day, I might *not* come in
   For something handsome.

CHARLES HENRY LUDERS

A CORSAGE BOUQUET

MYRTILLA tonight
   Wears Jacqueminot roses.
She's the loveliest sight —
Myrtilla tonight!
Correspondingly light
   My pocketbook closes.
Myrtilla tonight
   Wears Jacqueminot roses.

CHARLES HENRY LUDERS

ACROSS THE FIELDS TO ANNE

How often in the summer-tide,
His graver business set aside,
Has stripling Will, the thoughtful-eyed,
   As to the pipes of Pan
Stepped blithesomely with lover's pride
   Across the fields to Anne!

It must have been a merry mile,
This summer stroll by hedge and stile,
With sweet foreknowledge all the while
   How sure the pathway ran
To dear delights of kiss and smile,
   Across the fields to Anne.

The silly sheep that graze to-day,
I wot, they let him go his way,
Nor once looked up, as who should say:
   'It is a seemly man.'
For many lads went wooing aye
   Across the fields to Anne.

The oaks, they have a wiser look;
Mayhap they whispered to the brook:
'The world by him shall yet be shook,
   It is in nature's plan;
Though now he fleets like any rook
   Across the fields to Anne.'

And I am sure, that on some hour
Coquetting soft 'twixt sun and shower,

He stooped and broke a daisy-flower
    With heart of tiny span,
And bore it as a lover's dower
    Across the fields to Anne.

While from her cottage garden-bed
She plucked a jasmine's goodlihede,
To scent his jerkin's brown instead;
    Now since that love began,
What luckier swain than he who sped
    Across the fields to Anne?

The winding path whereon I pace,
The hedgerows green, the summer's grace,
Are still before me face to face;
    Methinks I almost can
Turn poet and join the singing race
    Across the fields to Anne!

RICHARD BURTON

IN PRISON

DEAR maid! put your head on my breast, you will hear
    The prisoner drearily pacing his cell —
What's this? does he stumble or dream you are near,
    Or dreaming you near does he stumble as well?

For twenty long years in the gloom I have heard
    The prisoner's footsteps — for twenty or more —
Life-sentence it is — and he never has stirred
    From his steady strong tramp till this hour before.

Dear maid! put your ear to my breast, you will hear
  The prisoner knock in the gloom of his cell —
How he strikes on the walls, in his frenzy and fear,
  Lest you go and not hear what he wishes to tell!

FREDERICK PETERSON

THISBE

THE garden within was shaded,
  And guarded about from sight;
The fragrance flowed to the south wind,
  The fountain leaped to the light.

And the street without was narrow,
  And dusty and hot and mean;
But the bush that bore white roses,
  She leaned to the fence between.

And softly she sought a crevice
  In that barrier blank and tall,
And shyly she thrust out through it
  The loveliest bud of all.

And tender to touch, and gracious,
  And pure as the moon's pure shine,
The full rose paled and was perfect, —
  For whose eyes, for whose lips, but mine!

HELEN GRAY CONE

THE TENDER HEART

SHE gazed upon the burnished brace
  Of plump ruffed grouse he showed with pride;
Angelic grief was in her face:
  'How *could* you do it, dear?' she sighed.
'The poor, pathetic, moveless wings!
  The songs all hushed — oh, cruel shame!'
Said he, 'The partridge never sings.'
  Said she, 'The sin is quite the same.

'You men are savage through and through.
  A boy is always bringing in
Some string of bird's eggs, white and blue,
  Or butterfly upon a pin.
The angle-worm in anguish dies,
  Impaled, the pretty trout to tease —'
'My own, *I* fish for trout with flies —'
  'Don't wander from the question, please!'

She quoted Burns's 'Wounded Hare,'
  And certain burning lines of Blake's,
And Ruskin on the fowls of air,
  And Coleridge on the water-snakes.
At Emerson's 'Forbearance' he
  Began to feel his will benumbed;
At Browning's 'Donald' utterly
  His soul surrendered and succumbed.

'Oh, gentlest of all gentle girls,'
  He thought, 'beneath the blessed sun!'

He saw her lashes hung with pearls,
  And swore to give away his gun.
She smiled to find her point was gained,
  And went, with happy parting words
(He subsequently ascertained)
  To trim her hat with humming-birds.

HELEN GRAY CONE

LENTEN LINES TO LYDIA

LYDIA, now that days are ashen,
  And 'tis fashion to repent,
Must I curb my manly passion
  Till the end of Lent?
You've forsworn — how well I know it —
  All the folly of the throng;
Prithee, don't forswear your poet
  And his song!

Lydia, dearest, should you do so,
  I should be immersed in woes;
Like a maid without a trousseau,
  I'd have 'indigoes.'
Gray would streak my locks of raven,
  I should lose my youthful air;
On my heart would be engraven
  Deep — *despair!*

Lydia, show some gentle feeling!
  Here, with fervor, I repeat

That I'm (figuratively) kneeling
  At your pretty feet.
Do not drive me to the doctor
  For some bitter draught to sup!
How could any pill-concocter
  Buoy me up?

Lydia, Lydia, be tender!
  Pity me, and hear my plea!
You might send your heart's surrender
  In epitome!
One brief word would so delight me;
  (Just below is my address!)
Lydia loveliest, O write me! —
  Tell me 'yes!'

Address me at The Rhymer's Quill;
The Muses' Street, Parnassus Hill.
                              SENNETT STEPHENS

CHLORIS AND CORYDON

CHLORIS, a maid of nimble feet,
  Whose tongue was nimble too,
A shepherd, — Corydon, I weet, —
  Came bashfully to woo.

He spoke with awkward turn of head,
  A-leaning on his crook,
'Now get thee gone,' the maiden said,
  'Thou hast a sheepish look!'

174

At this in tender tone he sighed,
   'In love with thee I am';
And she in merry laughter cried,
   'It is a pretty lamb!'

Then roared he out, a lion bold,
   His love of many a day,
Until sweet Chloris, it is told,
   Was glad to say him 'yea.'

Thus maids in pastoral days were won,
   Are still — my tale is true;
For I was shepherd Corydon,
   And Chloris — that was you!

SENNETT STEPHENS

ASTROLOGY

I USED to delve in classic lore,
   Con Plato's great 'Apology,'
Explore the many myths of yore,
   And revel in Astrology.
To look into the vault of blue
   With reverence each night I went;
I ranged celestial meadows through,
   Then home in chilly plight I went.

I gazed at Great and Little Bear
   And saw in each of them an eye;

Discovered many wonders rare
   In Capricorn and Gemini.
I knew the rites and symbols known
   In times of haughty Ptolemy,
And when I talked in learned tone
   Scarce any man could follow me.

My vision fell one happy day
   Upon a maiden — Claribel;
I was a slave beneath her sway,
   I'd never seen so fair a belle.
And from the hour I met her eyes
   (I say this in apology)
I found in them the clearest skies
   To study my Astrology.

SENNETT STEPHENS

A WINTER'S TALE

WHEN thick and fast the snow flies
   And winter's dream comes true,
Straight as the hungry crow flies
   My Fancy goes to you;
Across the miles to greet you, —
   Love's one unchanging star, —
And say again how sweet you
   Are.

The wings of Hope are tireless,
   The heart of Love is gay;

Our messages were wireless
  Before Marconi's day;
And Fancy has no fear you
  Have made the flight so far
He cannot tell how dear you
  Are.

The white flakes have no terror
  For Love whose compass shows
The way without an error
  To you, my winter rose;
So when he comes to bless you
  And call you mine, don't mar
My dream, but just confess you
  Are!

FRANK DEMPSTER SHERMAN

AN UNTUTORED MIND

WHEN I was but a lad of eight,
  And Dorothy was turning seven,
My life seemed spent close by the gate
  Of what I had imagined Heaven;
So sweet was Dorothy, and mild,
  To every fault of mine so tender,
I grew to love her as a child
  Accustomed always to befriend her.

Through school hours I observed her dress. —
  Plain calico to me was satin;

The habit often cost recess
    And many weary lines of Latin.
She very seldom turned her face,
    Replete with roses, fair and ruddy;
She seemed to think the school a place
    For strict deportment and for study.

In all the classes she was first;
    She graduated, — went to college, —
Returned most wonderfully versed
    In every branch and twig of knowledge.
Alas, I wear no savant's cap!
    My brain is not a book-condenser!
No doubt she'll marry that young chap
    I hear her call 'Dear Herbert Spencer!'
                        FRANK DEMPSTER SHERMAN

IN PARENTHESIS

I READ the verses from my copy,
    A bunch of fancies culled from Keats,
A rhyme of rose and drowsy poppy,
    Of maiden, song, and other sweets;
The lines — so patiently I penned them,
    Without one sable blot or blur —
I knew had music to commend them
    And all their secret thoughts to her.

She heard the rhythmical romanza,
    And made a comment there and here;

I read on to the final stanza,
   Where timid love had made me fear.
A long parenthesis; the metre
   Went lamely on without a foot,
Because the sentiment was sweeter
   Than love emboldened me to put.

Alas, I tried to fill the bracket;
   The truant thought refused to come!
The point, — to think the rhyme should lack it!
   My wakeful conscience struck me dumb.
She took the little leaf a minute, —
   Ah, what a happy time was this!
The bracket soon had something in it, —
   I kissed her in parenthesis.

FRANK DEMPSTER SHERMAN

A BUNDLE OF LETTERS

STRANGE how much sentiment
Clings like a fragrant scent
To these love-letters pent
   In their pink covers:
Day after day they came
Feeding love's fickle flame; —
Now, she has changed her name, —
   Then we were lovers.

Loosen the silken band
Round the square bundle, and

See what a dainty hand
　　Scribbled to fill it
Full of facetious chat;
Fancy how long she sat
Moulding the bullets that
　　Came with each billet!

Ah, I remember still
Time that I used to kill
Waiting the postman's shrill,
　　Heart-stirring whistle,
Calling vague doubts to mind,
Whether or no I'd find
That he had left behind
　　One sweet epistle.

Seconds become an age
At this exciting stage;
Two eager eyes the page
　　Scan for a minute;
Then, with true lover's art,
Study it part by part,
Until they know by heart
　　Everything in it.

Criss-cross the reading goes,
Rapturous rhyme and prose, —
Words which I don't suppose
　　Look very large in
Books on the 'ologies';

Then there's a tiny frieze
Full of sweets in a squeeze
    Worked on the margin.

Lastly, — don't pause to laugh! —
That is her autograph
Signing this truce for half
    Her heart's surrender;
Post-scriptum, one and two, —
Desserts, — the dinner's through! —
Linking the 'I' and 'You'
    In longings tender.

Such is the type of all
Save one, and let me call
Brief notice to this small
    Note neatly written:
'Tis but a card, you see,
Gently informing me
That it can never be! —
    This is the mitten!

                    FRANK DEMPSTER SHERMAN

BROKER CUPID

CUPID is my Broker,
    So to him I went
When my sweetheart spoke her
    Mind on sentiment.

One could not deny it —
  Straight from Love's red lips,
So I bade him buy it
  On her tips.

In his office cozy,
  With the sign above
Writ in letters rosy,
  'Stocks and Bonds of Love.'
Here I watch the Ticker
  For my stock to climb;
And my heart beats quicker
  Every time.

Thirty, forty, fifty;
  Better every day!
I am getting thrifty
  In a pleasant way.
Dividends of kisses
  Frequently declared,
And abundant blisses
  Freely shared.

There's no need to borrow;
  Mine's a lucky star!
Cupid says tomorrow
  Love will go to Par.
Sweetheart, since you let a
  Fellow grow so fond,

I think now I'll get a
Marriage Bond!

FRANK DEMPSTER SHERMAN

HER FAULTS

My sweetheart has her faults in plenty,
  Which I perceive with much distress;
For instance, she is only twenty,
  And one would think her even less;
While I may mention it between us —
  (Excuse the confidence betrayed) —
Her form is plagiarized from Venus,
  And no acknowledgment is made.
Her hair is much too fine and curly;
  Her lips are merely Cupid's bow;
Her teeth absurdly white and pearly;
  But still we all have faults, you know.

So, spite of this and spite of that,
  Whate'er betide, whate'er befall,
These things let others cavil at;
  I love my sweetheart, faults and all.

From such defects this little lady
  Of mine is anything but free.
Her lashes are 'extremely shady,'
  Her eyes are 'much too deep for me.'
Two dimples have been thought too many
  For one small maiden to possess.

Her rivals wish she hadn't any;
  But what's a dimple more or less?
Her voice attracts o'ermuch attention
  Because of its melodious ring.
Her foot — but that I shall not mention —
  It's such a very little thing.

Yes, spite of that and spite of this,
  Whate'er betide, whate'er befall,
Though others may perfection miss,
  I love my sweetheart, faults and all.

HARRY B. SMITH

BE YE IN LOVE WITH APRIL–TIDE

Be ye in love with April-tide?
    I' faith, in love am I!
  For now 'tis sun, and now 'tis shower,
  And now 'tis frost, and now 'tis flower,
And now 'tis Laura laughing-eyed,
    And now 'tis Laura shy!

Ye doubtful days, oh, slower glide!
    Still smile and frown, O sky!
  Some beauty unforeseen I trace
  In every change of Laura's face; —
Be ye in love with April-tide?
    I' faith, in love am I!

CLINTON SCOLLARD

RETICENT LOVER

I DARE not sing my lady's praise
About the world's wide wander-ways
Lest unbelievers should declare
That there is none so fond and fair,
And I be angered, knowing she
Is fairer than the fairest be.

I dare not speak my lady's name
Lest other lovers should proclaim
Their loves, and in my deafened ears
Drown hers that has to me no peers,
Knowing her name is sweeter far
Than names of any others are.

I dare not laud my lady's love,
The luring tenderness thereof,
Lest some one flout, and straightway say
That Helen loved once on a day,
And white Iseult, and yet I know
Like my own love they loved not so.

CLINTON SCOLLARD

DAFFODIL TIME

IT is daffodil time, so the robins all cry,
For the sun's a big daffodil up in the sky,
And when down the midnight the owl calls 'to-whoo'!
Why, then the round moon is a daffodil too;

Now sheer to the bough-tops the sap starts to climb,
So, merry my masters, it's daffodil time!

It is time for the song; it is time for the sonnet;
It is time for Belinda to have a new bonnet,
All fashioned and furbished with things that are fair,
To rest like a crown on her daffodil hair;
Love beats in the heart like the pulse of a rhyme,
So, merry my masters, it's daffodil time!

It is time when the vales and the hills cry — 'away!
Come, join in the joy of the daffodil day!'
For somewhere one waits, with a glow on her face,
With her daffodil smile, and her daffodil grace.
There's a lilt in the air, there's a cheer, there's a chime,
So, merry my masters, it's daffodil time!

CLINTON SCOLLARD

DARLEY DALE

OH, I must be in Darley Dale before the sun dips low,
But can't tell, for the life of me, the way that I should
    go!
For if I take the one road there's Anabel to see,
And if I take the other road there is sweet Margery.

Within the eyes of Anabel there is a laughing lure;
The starry eyes of Margery are like the Cynosure;
Though Anabel's are larkspur-blue and Margery's are
    brown,

186

If I should think to drown myself, in both I'd like to
    drown.

The lovely lips of Anabel are like a crimson pink,
While Margery's seem a tulip cup that tempts a man to
    drink;
The hair of one has morning glints, the other's twilight
    hues;
The voice of each is melody. Pray, how am I to choose?

If Anabel starts marketing, the friendly grasses stir;
If Margery on an errand trips, the rushes bow to her;
Of both of them keep gossiping the leaves of every tree;
How can I tell if Anabel or Margery's for me?

Oh, I must be in Darley Dale before the sun dips low,
But can't say, for the heart of me, the way that I should go!
                CLINTON SCOLLARD

A NAME FOR MY LOVE

IF there be truth in ancient saws
    It surely would be meet
That I should call my love 'Revenge';
    They say Revenge is sweet.

Or I might name her 'Conscience'
    Who makes cowards of us all;
Or her who teaches more than books,
    'Experience' I might call.

'Economy is wealth,' they say,
  She's wealth enough for me.
'Consistency's a jewel,' and
  A jewel too is she.

And yet sometimes she drives me mad,
  So 'Learning' would be fit,
And she'd do grace to 'Brevity'
  For she's the soul of wit.

Yet when before her varied charms
  My suppliant knee is bent,
I'd rather call her 'Silence' for
  'Tis Silence gives consent.

W. K. WELSH

LOVER LOQUITUR

LIEGE lady! believe me,
  All night, from my pillow
I heard, but to grieve me,
  The plash of the willow;
The rain on the towers,
  The winds without number,
In the gloom of the hours,
  And denial of slumber.

And nigh to the dawning, —
  My heart aching blindly,
Unresting and mourning
  That you were unkindly, —

What did I ostensibly,
  Ah, what under heaven,
Liege lady! but sensibly
  Doze till eleven?

LOUISE IMOGEN GUINEY

PRIVATE THEATRICALS

You were a haughty beauty, Polly,
  (That was in the play,)
I was the lover melancholy;
  (That was in the play.)
And when your fan and you receded,
And all my passion lay unheeded,
If still with tenderer words I pleaded,
  That was in the play.

I met my rival at the gateway,
  (That was in the play,)
And so we fought a duel straightway;
  (That was in the play.)
But when Jack hurt my arm unduly,
And you rushed over, softened newly,
And kissed me, Polly! truly, truly,
  Was that in the play?

LOUISE IMOGEN GUINEY

CONSOLATION

DEAR Betty, when an hour ago
  You scorned my humble offer
Because my lean and empty purse
  Was not a well-filled coffer,
Why did you breathe your cruel 'No'
  With such a frightened quiver?
Perhaps you thought I meant to seek
  Some suicidal river.

Ah, no, sweet girl! These modern times
  Of cynic calculation
Take wiser ways and means to end
  A lover's desperation;
And Corydon no longer sighs
  His heart away in sorrow,
But seeks a richer Phyllis out
  And woos again tomorrow.

MARY E. WILKINS

THE HAZARD

HE dared not ask a kiss
  For fear that she'd not brook it,
But, eager still for bliss,
  He boldly went and took it.

And now he's unaware
  If she did like or spurn it,

For she, right then and there,
Compelled him to return it.

JOHN KENDRICK BANGS

ON BEING GOOD

IT is not easy to be good
At all times as one really should.
Temptations lie on every hand
That only saints can well withstand.
E'en though to virtue one's inclined,
Old Satan will not stay behind.

One thing, however, is quite sure —
In one Commandment I'm secure.
Since Daphne came to live next door,
I find it difficult no more —
Stop laughing, Cupid! Naughty Elf! —
To love my neighbor as myself!

JOHN KENDRICK BANGS

THE OLD COLLECTOR

'TIS strange to look across the street
And feel that we no more shall meet
Our middle-aged, precise, and neat
    Old-fashioned neighbor.
It seems, in his unlighted hall,
His much-prized pictures on the wall

Must miss his presence, and recall
    His loving labor.

His manner was serene and fine,
Fashioned on some Old-World design.
His wit grew keener with the wine,
    And kindlier after;
And when the revelry rang high,
No one could make more apt reply;
Yet, though they sometimes marked his sigh,
    None heard his laughter.

He held as foolish him who dotes
On politics or petticoats;
He vowed he'd hear no talk of votes
    Or silly scandals.
No journeys tempted him; he swore
He held his world within his door,
And there he'd dwell till life was o'er,
    Secure from vandals.

'Why should I roam the world again?'
He said. 'Domingo shows me Spain;
The dust of travel then were vain.
    What springtime chances
To match my Corot there! One glance
Is worth a year of actual France.
The real ne'er equals the romance,
    Nor fact our fancies.'

192

His walls were decked with maidens fair —
A Henner with rich auburn hair;
A Reynolds with the stately air
    That fits a beauty;
There glanced a Greuze with girlish grace;
And yonder, with the strong, calm face,
The peasant sister of her race,
    Whose life is duty.

He valued most the sunny day
Because it lighted his Dupré,
And showed his small Meissonier
    In proper fashion.
And tender was the glance he bent
Upon his missal's ornament,
Whereon some patient monk had spent
    His artist passion.

I used to love to see him pass
His fingers o'er some rare old glass.
He never took delight *en masse*;
    He loved each treasure:
The precious bronzes from Japan,
The rugs from towered Ispahan,
His rose-tint Sèvres, his famous fan —
    Each had its pleasure.

And so he held that Art was all;
Yet when Death made the solemn call,
Before the desk in his long hall
    They found him sitting.

Within the hands clasped on his breast
An old daguerreotype was pressed —
A sweet-faced, smiling girl, and dressed
    In frills befitting.

Naught of his story can we know,
Nor whose the fault so long ago,
Nor with what meed of weal or woe
    His love was blended.
Yet o'er his rare Delft mantel-tiles
Bellini's sweet Madonna smiles
As though she knew the weary miles
    For him are ended.

BEATRICE HANSCOM

FEAR

THERE is a sound I would not hear,
    Although it music's self might be;
Lest in my breast a crystal sphere
    Might burst, might break for melody.

There is a face I would not see
    Though like the springtime it were fair;
Lest love that was a barren tree
    Should burst in bloom — should blossoms bear.

LANGDON ELWYN MITCHELL

IN ABSENCE

THE sky is blue, is blue, today,
The landward hills are green, men say:
I do not know, I cannot see,
For I am blind away from thee.

Men say the breakers stoop and run,
Loud laughing in the noonday sun:
I do not know, I cannot hear,
For I am deaf, save thou art near.

The coverts of the live-oaks sing,
Men say, with tuning notes of Spring:
For me Spring is not yet — thou art
The absent April of my heart.

ROBERT CAMERON ROGERS

TO ARCADY

ACROSS the hills of Arcady
  Into the Land of Song —
Ah, dear, if you will go with me
  The way will not be long!

It does not lie through solitudes
  Of wind-blown woods or sea;
Dear, no! The city's weariest moods
  May scarce veil Arcady.

'Tis in no unfamiliar land
  Lit by some distant star;

195

See! Arcady is where you stand,
   And song is where you are.

Then go but hand in hand with me —
   No road can lead us wrong;
Here are the hills of Arcady —
   This is the Land of Song.

CHARLES BUXTON GOING

LOVE'S DETECTIVE

THEY always called her Love's detective,
   Thought her inopportune, but harmless.
She looked at life without perspective,
   A dry soul, erudite and charmless.

She had a habit of appearing
   Just when four lips were ripe for kissing.
'Excuse me if I'm interfering.'
   The mild words sounded like a hissing.

And when at last the bomb exploded
   Which rent love like a wind-blown thistle,
They never knew that she had loaded,
   And primed, and aimed, and fired the missile.

GAMALIEL BRADFORD

CAN'T YOU

Oh, believe I wish you well!
  But I will not haunt you,
Lie awake devising spell
  Or potion to enchant you.
Since I know that charms divine
  Cannot move or daunt you,
Go your way and I'll go mine.
  Leave me peaceful — can't you?

GAMALIEL BRADFORD

A POSSIBILITY

I only kissed her hand;
  Is that why Lisette dislikes me?
I cannot understand —
I only kissed her hand,
I deserved a reprimand; —
  But another notion strikes me:
I only kissed her *hand*;
  Is that why Lisette dislikes me?

CAROLYN WELLS

CUPID'S FAILURE

Cupid one day, in idle quest,
  Fitted a dainty dart
And aimed it at Priscilla's breast,
  To strike Priscilla's heart.

Clean through it went, no heart was there;
　　Said Cupid, 'I believe
Priscilla's just the girl to wear
　　Her heart upon her sleeve.'

But there, alack, it was not found!
　　'Aha!' cried Cupid, 'note
Her frightened air; now I'll be bound
　　Her heart is in her throat.'

Failure again. On slender chance
　　He one more arrow shoots;
Assuming from her downcast glance
　　Her heart is in her boots.

Foiled, Cupid threw away his bow;
　　'She has no heart,' said he.
(He did not know that long ago
　　She gave her heart to me.)

CAROLYN WELLS

A SONG

Upon a time I had a Heart,
And it was bright and gay
I gave it to a Lady fair
To have and keep alway.

She soothed it and she smoothed it
And she stabbed it till it bled;

She brightened it and lightened it
And she weighed it down with lead.

She flattered it and battered it
And she filled it full of gall;
Yet had I Twenty Hundred Hearts,
Still she should have them all.

OLIVER HERFORD

THE POET'S PROPOSAL

PHYLLIS, if I could paint you
  As I see you sitting there,
You distracting little saint, you,
  With your aureole of hair,
If I only *were* an artist,
  And such glances could be caught,
You should have the very smartest
  Picture frame that can be bought.

Phyllis, since I can't depict your
  Charms, or give you aught but fame,
Will you be yourself the picture?
  Will you let me be the frame?
Whose protecting clasp may bind you
  Always —
            'Nay,' cried Phyllis, 'hold,
Or you'll force me to remind you
  Paintings *must* be framed with gold!'

OLIVER HERFORD

MRS. GOLIGHTLY

THE time is come to speak, I think,
  For on the square I met
My beauteous widow, fresh and pink,
Her black gown touched at every brink
  With tender violet;

And at her throat the white *crepe lisse*
  Spoke, in a fluffy bow,
Of woe that should perhaps ne'er cease —
(Peace to thy shade, Golightly, peace!)
  Yet mitigated woe.

In her soft eye, that used to scan
  The ground, nor seem to see,
The hazel legend sweetly ran,
'I *could* not wholly hate a man
  For quite adoring me.'

And when she drew her kerchief fine,
  A hint of heliotrope
Its snow edged with an inky line
Exhaled, — from which scent you divine
  Through old regrets new hope.

And then her step, so soft and slow,
  She scarcely seemed to lift
From off the sward her widowed toe, —
One year, one little year ago! —
  So soft yet, yet so swift.

Then, too, her blush, her side glance coy,
  Tell me in easy Greek
(I wonder could her little boy
Prove source of serious annoy?)
  The time has come to speak.

GERTRUDE HALL

APPLIED ASTRONOMY

HE took me out to see the stars,
  That astronomic bore;
He said there were two moons near Mars,
  While Jupiter had four.

I thought of course he'd whisper soon
  What fourfold bliss 'twould be
To stroll beneath that fourfold moon
  Of Jupiter with me.

And when he spoke of Saturn's ring,
  I was convinced he'd say
That was the very kind of thing
  To offer me some day.

But in a tangent off he went
  To double stars. Now that
Was most suggestive, so content
  And quite absorbed I sat.

But no, he talked a dreamy mess,
  Of which the only fraction

That caught my fancy, I confess,
  Was 'mutual attraction.'

I said I thought it very queer
  And stupid altogether,
For stars to keep so very near
  And yet not come together.

At that he smiled, and turned his head;
  I thought he'd caught the notion;
He merely bowed good-night and said —
  Their safety lay in motion.

ESTHER B. TIFFANY

THE LOVE OF A BOY

HEIGH-HO! my thoughts are far away;
For wine or books I have no care;
I like to think upon the way
She has of looking very fair.
  Oh, work is nought, and play is nought,
  And all the livelong day is nought;
  There's nothing much I care to learn
  But what her lovely lips have taught.

The campus cannot tempt me out;
The classics cannot keep me in;
The only place I care about
Is where perchance she may have been.
  Oh, work is nought, and play is nought,

And all the livelong day is nought;
There's nothing much I care to find
Except the way she would be sought.

The train across the valley screams,
And like a hawk sweeps out of sight;
It bears me to her in my dreams
By day and night, by day and night.
  Oh, work is nought, and play is nought,
  And all the livelong day is nought;
  There's nothing much I care to be,
  If I be only in her thought.

RICHARD HOVEY

UNFORESEEN

WHY did I kiss you, sweet?
Nor you nor I can say.
You might have said some commonplace,
I might have turned away.

No thought was in our hearts
Of what we were to be.
Fate sent a madness on our souls
And swept us out to sea.

Fate, between breath and breath,
Has made the world anew,
And the bare skies of yesterday
Are all aflame with you.

RICHARD HOVEY

REED CALL

When April comes, and pelts with buds
  And apple-blooms each orchard space,
And takes the dogwood-whitened woods
With rain and sunshine of her moods,
    Like your fair face, like your sweet face:
      It's honey for the bud and dew,
        And honey for the heart!
      And, oh, to be away with you
        Beyond the town and mart!

When April comes and tints the hills
  With gold and beryl that rejoice,
And from her airy apron spills
The laughter of the winds and rills,
    Like your young voice, like your sweet voice:
      It's gladness for God's bending blue,
        And gladness for the heart!
      And, oh, to be away with you
        Beyond the town and mart!

When April comes, and binds and girds
  The world with warmth that breathes above,
And to the breeze flings all her birds,
Whose songs are welcome as the words
    Of you I love, O you I love:
      It's music for all things that woo,
        And music for the heart!
      And, oh, to be away with you
        Beyond the town and mart!

                              MADISON CAWEIN

LOVE AND A DAY

Of honey and heat and weed and wheat
  The day had made perfume;
And Heaven a tower of turquoise raised,
Whence Noon, like some pale woman, gazed —
A sunflower withered at her waist —
  Within a crystal room.

Said I to Love: 'What must I do?
What shall I do? what can I do?'
Said I to Love: 'What must I do,
  All in the summer nooning?'

Said Love to me: 'Go woo! go woo!'
  Said Love to me: 'Go woo!
If she be 'mid the rakers, O!
Among the harvest acres, O!
While every breeze brings scents of hay,
Just hold her hand and not take "nay,"
  All in the summer nooning!'

MADISON CAWEIN

LYDIA

When Autumn's here and days are short,
  Let Lydia laugh, and, hey,
Straightway 'tis May-day in my heart,
  And blossoms strew the way!

When Summer's here and days are long,
  Let Lydia sigh and, ho,

December's fields I walk among,
    And shiver in the snow!

No matter what the seasons are,
    My Lydia is so dear,
My heart admits no calendar
    Of earth when she is near.

MADISON CAWEIN

DIGHTON IS ENGAGED

DIGHTON is engaged! Think of it and tremble!
Two-and-twenty ladies who have known him must dis-
        semble;
Two-and-twenty ladies in a panic must repeat,
'Dighton is a gentleman; will Dighton be discreet?'
All the merry maidens who have known him at his best
Wonder what the girl is like, and if he has confessed.
    Dighton the philanderer, will he prove a slanderer?
A man gets confidential ere the honeymoon has sped —
    Dighton was a rover then, Dighton lived in clover
        then;
Dighton is a gentleman — but Dighton is to wed!

Dighton is engaged! Think of it, Corinna!
Watch and see his fiancée smile on you at dinner!
Watch and hear his fiancée whisper, '*That's* the one?'
Try and raise a blush for what you said was 'only fun.'
Long have you been wedded; have you then forgot?

If you have, I'll venture that a certain man has not!
Dighton had a way with him; did you ever play with
him?
Now that dream is over and the episode is dead.
Dighton never harried you after Charlie married you;
Dighton is a gentleman — but Dighton is to wed!

Dighton is engaged! Think of it, Bettina!
Did you ever love him when the sport was rather
keener?
Did you ever kiss him as you sat upon the stairs?
Did you ever tell him of your former love affairs?
Think of it uneasily and wonder if his wife
Soon will know the amatory secrets of your life!
Dighton was impressible, you were quite accessible —
The bachelor who marries late is apt to lose his head.
Dighton wouldn't hurt you; does it disconcert you?
Dighton is a gentleman — but Dighton is to wed!

Dighton is engaged! Tremble, Mrs. Alice!
When he comes no longer will you bear the lady malice?
Now he comes to dinner, and he smokes cigars with
Clint,
But he never makes a blunder and he never drops a hint;
He's a universal uncle, with a welcome everywhere,
He adopts his sweetheart's children and he lets 'em pull
his hair.
Dighton has a memory bright and sharp as emery,
He could tell them fairy stories that would make you
rather red!

Dighton can be trusted, though; Dighton's read-
justed, though!
Dighton is a gentleman — but Dighton is to wed!

GELETT BURGESS

PHILLIS AND CORYDON

PHILLIS took a red rose from the tangles of her hair, —
Time, the Golden Age; the place, Arcadia, anywhere, —

Phillis laughed, the saucy jade: 'Sir Shepherd, wilt have
this,
Or' — Bashful god of skipping lambs and oaten reeds!
— 'a kiss?'

Bethink thee, gentle Corydon! A rose lasts all night
long,
A kiss but slips from off your lips like a thrush's evening
song.

A kiss that goes, where no one knows! A rose, a crimson
rose!
Corydon made his choice and took — Well, which do
you suppose?

ARTHUR COLTON

CONCERNING TABITHA'S DANCING OF THE MINUET

TABITHA, sweet Tabitha, I never can forget,
Nor how the music sounded, nor how our glances met,
When underneath the swinging lamps we danced the
minuet.

The stately bow, the dainty poise, and in the music
slips.
Did she linger for a moment, while I held her finger tips,
And wondered if she'd ever let me touch them to my
lips?

And Tabitha wore powdered hair and dressed in quaint
brocade,
A tiny patch on either cheek just where the dimple
played;
The little shoe I noticed too, and clocks, I am afraid.

The music ceased. I led her softly smiling to the door.
A pause, a rustling courtesy down almost to the floor,
And Tabitha, sweet Tabitha, mine eyes beheld no more.

I've trod in many measures since with widow, wife, and
maid,
In every kind of satin, silk, and spangled lace arrayed,
And through it all have heard the fall of Tabitha's
brocade.

ARTHUR COLTON

LOVE TRIUMPHANT

Helen's lips are drifting dust;
Ilion is consumed with rust;
All the galleons of Greece
Drink the ocean's dreamless peace,
Lost was Solomon's purple show
Restless centuries ago;
Stately empires wax and wane —
Babylon, Barbary, and Spain; —
Only one thing, undefaced,
Lasts, though all the worlds lie waste
And the heavens are overturned.
— Dear, how long ago we learned!

There's a sight that blinds the sun,
Sound that lives when sounds are done,
Music that rebukes the birds,
Language lovelier than words,
Hue and scent that shame the rose,
Wine no earthly vineyard knows,
Silence stiller than the shore
Swept by Charon's stealthy oar,
Ocean more divinely free
Than Pacific's boundless sea, —
Ye who love have learned it true.
— Dear, how long ago we knew!

FREDERIC LAWRENCE KNOWLES

A SONG OF CONTENT

How many million stars must shine
    Which only God can see! —
Yet in the sky His hand has hung
    Ten thousand stars for me!

How many blossoms bloom and fade
    Which only God can know! —
Yet here's my field of buttercups,
    And here my daisies blow.

How many wing-paths through the blue
    Lure swallows up and down —
Yet here's my little garden walk,
    And yon's the road to town!

How many a treacherous voice has wooed
    Unhappy feet to roam —
Yet God has taught my willing ear
    The sounds of *love* and *home!*

How many lips have kissed and clung
    Since Eve was Adam's bride! —
But God has given me you, dear girl,
    And I am satisfied!

FREDERIC LAWRENCE KNOWLES

MY LADY GOES TO THE PLAY

WITH link-boys running on before
   To light her on her way,
A-lounging in her sedan goes
   Belinda to the play.

In patch and powder, puff and frill,
   From satin shoe to hair,
Of all the maids in London town
   I wot there's none so fair!

From Mayfair down along the Strand
   To Covent Garden's light,
Where Master David Garrick acts
   In a new rôle tonight,

The swinging sedan takes its way,
   And with expectant air
Belinda fans, and wonders who
   Tonight there will be there.

Sir Charles, perhaps, or, happy thought,
   Flushing through her powder,
He might come in — beneath her stays
   She feels her heart beat louder.

The place at last! The flunkies set
   Their dainty burden down.
'Lud, what a crowd!' My Lady frowns
   And gathers up her gown.

Alack for human loveliness
  And for its little span!
Where is Belinda? Here, quite fresh,
  Are still her gown and fan!

                   ARTHUR KETCHUM

BOUTON D'OR

Up at Forclaz, on the Pass,
  Picking *bouton d'or*,
Watching how the mountains stand
  Round the dark Tête Noire,

You and I, in flush of youth,
  Comrades of a day,
Looked the look one can't forget —
  Then we went our way.

Where you are now — heaven knows,
  Comrade of a day;
Have you found one who can hold
  Looks like that for aye?

Or do you too sometimes pause
  And wish yourself once more
Up at Forclaz, on the Pass
  Picking *bouton d'or*?

             JESSIE B. RITTENHOUSE

PARADOX

I WENT out to the woods today
  To hide away from you,
From you a thousand miles away —
  But you came, too.

And yet the old dull thought would stay,
  And all my heart benumb —
If you were but a mile away
  You would not come.

JESSIE B. RITTENHOUSE

COMMUNION

Cows beneath a great oak tree,
  One neck folded on another,
What superb complacency
  In a world where humans smother!

What communion in each breath,
  Passing days in dumb review,
While lovers talk themselves to death
  And remain forever two.

JESSIE B. RITTENHOUSE

A MORAL IN SÈVRES

UPON my mantel-piece they stand,
  While all its length between them lies;
He throws a kiss with graceful hand,
  She glances back with bashful eyes.

The china Shepherdess is fair,
    The Shepherd's face denotes a heart
Burning with ardor and despair.
    Alas, they stand so far apart!

And yet, perhaps, if they were moved,
    And stood together day by day,
Their love had not so constant proved,
    Nor would they still have smiled so gay.

His hand the Shepherd might have kissed
    The match-box Angel's heart to win;
The Shepherdess, his love have missed,
    And flirted with the Mandarin.

But on my mantel-piece they stand,
    While all its length between them lies;
He throws a kiss with graceful hand,
    She glances back with bashful eyes.

                              MILDRED HOWELLS

BANQUET SONG

COMRADES, fill the banquet cup
    Brimming up!
Fill it full of love and laughter,
Claret lips and kisses after;
Crown it with a maiden's smiles,
And the foam of magic wiles.

215

Drink it, drain it, clink your glasses,
For the love of loving lasses
　Ere it passes!

Fill again the banquet cup
　Brimming up!
Overflow it with the roses,
Which her timid blush discloses.
With her sparkling eyelight sift it,
Till it flavored is. Then lift it.
Drink it, drain it, clink your glasses,
For the love of loving lasses
　Ere it passes!

Comrades, fill a parting cup
　Brimming up!
Flood it in your praise's zest
For the uninvited guest.
With her charms and graces fill it,
Touch the lips and heart-ward spill it.
Drink it, drain it, clink your glasses,
For the love of loving lasses
　Ere it passes!

EDWIN OSGOOD GROVER

THIS IS SHE

On order that must be obeyed
I sing of a dear little maid;
   A mirthfully serious,
   Sober, delerious,
   Gently imperious
     Maid.

And first we'll consider her eyes
(Alike as to color and size);
   Her winkable, blinkable,
   Merrily twinkable,
   Simply unthinkable
     Eyes.

Then, having a moment to spare,
We turn our attention to hair;
   Her tendrilly-curlative,
   Tumbly-and-whirlative,
   Super-superlative
     Hair.

Forbear to dismiss with a shrug
Her nose, undeniably pug; —
   Her strictly permissable,
   Turn-up-like-thisable,
   Urgently kissable
     Pug.

Now, moving a point to the south,
We come to an Actual Mouth;

A coral, pearliferous,
Argumentiferous,
Mainly melliferous
    Mouth.

Observe, underneath it, a chin,
Connoting the dimple within;
    A steady, reliable,
    Hardly defiable,
    True, undeniable
        Chin.

By all that is fair! it appears
We'd almost forgotten her ears!
    Those never neglectable,
    Tinted, delectable,
    Highly respectable
        Ears!

And last let us speak of herself,
That blithe little gipsy and elf,
    Her quite unignorable,
    Absence-deplorable,
    Wholly adorable
        Self.

                    ARTHUR GUITERMAN

218

A PLEA

STAMP not your little foot!
  My heart, my heart's below it;
For there my heart I put,
  And well, too well you know it.
A quarrel's aftermath,
  How long, too long it lingers.
In dire though lovely wrath
  Clench not your slender fingers,
They wring my soul!   Nor let
  The smile be longer missing
From lips in anger set
  That heaven made for kissing!

ARTHUR GUITERMAN

FASHION

FAIR Eve devised a walking-suit
  Of jungle grasses, soft and crimpy;
She thought it rather neat and cute
  Till Adam grunted, 'Pretty skimpy!'

A cloak of palm-leaves, sought for miles,
  She made, and came to be admired;
But Adam said, 'The silly styles
  You women wear just make me tired!'

She built herself a little hat
  Of lilies (Eve was *very* clever),

219

And asked him what he thought of *that?*
  And Adam blurted, 'Well, I *never!*'

So next she placed upon her head
  A feathered three-by-four Creation. —
The little word that Adam said
  Is barred from parlor conversation.

Yet Eve refused to be a dowd,
  And tied an autumn-tinted sash on.
'I'll dress to please *myself!*' she vowed,
  'For what does Adam know of fashion?'

'What use to seek applause from him?
  He scoffs and says I cannot reason!
Well, then, *my* law shall be my whim —
  And that shall change with every season.'

Since when, revolving cycles bring
  The gayest fashions and the queerest;
And Eve declares, 'It's just the thing!'
  And Adam murmurs, 'Is it, dearest?'

ARTHUR GUITERMAN

HIS WIDOW

THE wreaths shriveled and froze upon his grave.
She sat before the fire and warmed her knees
And yawned with relief and thought how black would
    please

The white of her skin; then softly trilled a stave
Of the new popular air, 'Life Isn't So Bad!'

A horrid day for a funeral!...But grief
Had certainly been becoming to her; and she
Had raised her veil at the prettiest time to see
Eyes bent upon her — men's eyes — ardent if brief.
She would be wealthy too... 'Life isn't so bad.'

She must reduce her hips though; and be brave
And sad; a second husband likes to take
A widow's weeds off — for a great new love's sake.
She knew just how she would let him — sweet and
        grave.
He should be very proud... 'Life isn't so bad.'

She brushed her hair and tended to her nails,
And ate a chocolate cream: the wreaths were freezing...
She cried a little; two or three tears came squeezing;
But told herself that true strength never fails
The deepest hearts, and ceased... 'Life isn't so bad.'

She went to bed. Her head upon the pillow
Would have looked very lovely, she was sure,
Had there been any one to see.... A year to endure!
She sighed, and felt as sad as wind in a willow,
And slept — and snored a little... Life isn't so bad.

CALE YOUNG RICE

SPADES

FORTY times I meant to dig
My grave — and never dug it.
Joy, the jade, would whisper, 'Wait:
Life has yet some nugget.'

So instead of graves I dug
Good ore — and lived to bury
Forty better men, who failed
To jilt Fate and be merry.

CALE YOUNG RICE

DINAH KNEADING DOUGH

I HAVE seen full many a sight
Born of day or drawn by night:
Sunlight on a silver stream,
Golden lilies all a-dream,
Lofty mountains, bold and proud,
Veiled beneath the lace-like cloud;
But no lovely sight I know
Equals Dinah kneading dough.

Brown arms buried elbow-deep
Their domestic rhythm keep,
As with steady sweep they go
Through the gently yielding dough.
Maids may vaunt their finer charms —
Naught to me like Dinah's arms;

Girls may draw, or paint, or sew —
I love Dinah kneading dough.

Eyes of jet and teeth of pearl,
Hair, some say, too tight a-curl;
But the dainty maid I deem
Very near perfection's dream.
Swift she works, and only flings
Me a glance — the least of things.
And I wonder, does she know
That my heart is in the dough?

PAUL LAURENCE DUNBAR

UNSAID

AH, lad, if I could only say
    The smiles are not for you!
But since your eyes are turned this way,
    What is there I can do?
It's one I see beyond, beyond,
    My heart is leaning to.

I know, I know, the whole hour long
    I have been dull and sad,
And answered not the word at all
    I meant to answer, lad;
Because my wits were gone astray
    With all the heart I had.

And now the latest ones are come,
    And he is coming too;

And I would keep the starlight back,
  But oh, it will shine through!
And since you never turn to see,
  You take it all to you.

JOSEPHINE PRESTON PEABODY

FORETHOUGHT

I DID not keep the rose he brought,
  After its day;
Although it lived a longer time
  Than other roses may.

I let it go the way of all
  For this one fear:
Because it might persuade my heart
  That he was growing dear.

But now my heart is well assured;
  And still I sing;
And no one here would ever know
  That I miss anything.

JOSEPHINE PRESTON PEABODY

THE CYNIC

I SAY it to comfort me over and over,
  Having a querulous heart to beguile,
Never had woman a tenderer lover —
  For a little while.

Oh, there never were eyes more eager to read her
    In her saddest mood or her moments gay,
Oh, there never were hands more strong to lead her —
    For a little way.

There never were loftier promises given
    Of love that should guard her the ages through,
As great, enduring and steadfast as Heaven —
    For a week or two.

Well, end as it does, I have had it, known it,
    For this shall I turn me to weep or pray?
Nay, rather I laugh that I thought to own it
    For more than a day.

                    THEODOSIA GARRISON

SHE WAS A CHILD OF FEBRUARY

SHE was a child of February,
    Of tree-top gray and smothered stream,
Of cedar and the marsh rosemary,
    Of snowbird and the sunset's dream.

A frozen brook that, April-eyed,
    Sings soft beneath its silver fretting,
Her lyric spirit soon belied
    The ice of her New England setting;

Till on a day when sudden thaw
    Rent all her snowy chains asunder,

The impassioned sun beheld with awe
  Her heart of deep Italian wonder.

Still Nature has described her best,
  Veiled in those February skies,
With summer singing in her breast,
  And April laughing in her eyes.

PERCY MACKAYE

THE ROSE FAMILY

THE rose is a rose,
And was always a rose.
But the theory now goes
That the apple's a rose,
And the pear is, and so's
The plum, I suppose.
The dear only knows
What will next prove a rose.
You, of course, are a rose —
But were always a rose.

ROBERT FROST

GRIEVE NOT, LADIES

OH, grieve not, Ladies, if at night
  Ye wake to feel your beauty going!
It was a web of frail delight,
  Inconstant as an April snowing.

In other eyes, in other lands,
　　In deep fair pools, new beauty lingers;
But like spent water in your hands
　　It runs from your reluctant fingers.

Ye shall not keep the singing lark
　　That owes to earlier skies its duty.
Weep not to hear along the dark
　　The sound of your departing beauty.

The fine and anguished ear of night
　　Is tuned to hear the smallest sorrow.
Oh, wait until the morning light!
　　It may not seem so gone tomorrow!

But honey-pale and rosy-red!
　　Brief lights that made a little shining!
Beautiful looks about us shed —
　　They leave us to the old repining.

Think not the watchful dim despair
　　Has come to you, the first, sweet-hearted!
For oh, the gold of Helen's hair!
　　And how she cried when that departed!

Perhaps that one that took the most,
　　The swiftest borrower, wildest spender,
May count, as we do not, the cost —
　　And grow more true to us and tender.

Happy are we if in his eyes
　　We see no shadow of forgetting.

Nay — if our star sinks in those skies
   We shall not wholly see its setting.

Then let us laugh as do the brooks
   That such immortal youth is ours,
If memory keeps for them our looks
   As fresh as are the spring-time flowers.

Oh, grieve not, Ladies, if at night
   Ye wake to feel the cold December!
Rather recall the early light
   And in your loved one's arms, remember.

ANNA HEMPSTEAD BRANCH

BEFORE THE FAIR

FROM the crow of the cock to the shut of the day
   I toiled most of any;
The cow and the flock and the load of hay
   From my few pence took many;
I worked all day in the sweat of my brow
   And only saved a penny.
     Here's a penny for my pretty,
      Sally needs an airing;
     She shall put a ribbon on
      And go to get a fairing!

Sally my girl so light she trips,
   And she laughs right out for glee;
And her warm lips are such red, red lips,
   And I won't be there to see —

228

But I'll get a promise from Sally my girl,
  That she'll kiss no lad but me.
    Here's a penny for my pretty,
      Sally needs an airing;
    She shall put a ribbon on
      And go to get a fairing!

Her crimson stocking is drawn so tight,
  Her ankle is plump and fair;
She'll lead the dance till the drop o' night
  With a posy in her hair.
And I can think as I turn my plough,
  My girl is the blithest there.
    Here's a penny for my pretty,
      Sally needs an airing;
    She shall put a ribbon on
      And go to get a fairing!

ANNA HEMPSTEAD BRANCH

HOW LIKE A WOMAN

I WANTED you to come today —
  Or so I told you in my letter —
And yet, if you had stayed away,
  I should have liked you so much better.
I should have sipped my tea unseen,
  And thrilled at every door-bell's pealing,
And thought how nice I could have been
  Had you evinced a little feeling.

I should have guessed you drinking tea
  With some one whom you loved to madness;
I should have thought you cold to me,
  And revelled in a depth of sadness.
But, no! you came without delay —
  I could not feel myself neglected:
You said the things you always say,
  In ways not wholly unexpected.

If you had let me wait in vain,
  We should, in my imagination,
Have held, what we did not attain,
  A most dramatic conversation.
Had you not come I should have known
  At least a vague anticipation,
Instead of which, I grieve to own,
  You did not give me one sensation.

CAROLINE AND ALICE DUER

PIERROT MAKES A SONG

FILLED with coquettish art,
  Blue-eyed and witty,
She of the fickle heart
  Is void of pity.

She of the frosty air,
  Whom love amuses,
Being so very fair
  Chills ere she chooses.

Who, given such a choice,
     Would not be chosen?
Who, knowing her, rejoice
     Not to be frozen?

Pierrette or Columbine?
     Which has the vision
Still to hold me divine,
     Or in derision?

WILLIAM GRIFFITH

ONE ROSE

I CANNOT bear the beauty of one rose;
Therefore, I pray you, give me two or three —
A nosegay of them, that my eye may be
Distracted, and not linger over-long
On one: its heart holds too much mystery.
Within it burn the holy vestal fires
Of all the world's deep longings and desires:
All loveliness is there! So soft among
Those tender petals such perfection glows,
I cannot bear the beauty of one rose.

MARY SINTON LEITCH

WHEN WE WERE POOR IN PARIS

WHEN we were poor in Paris
     In everything save Youth,
And the divine adventure,
     The magic quest of Truth,

Life held a glorious vision
  That riches cannot bring,
For I thought I was an artist,
  And you knew that you could sing.

When we were poor in Paris,
  (Ah! those were halcyon years,
With a crust a day for our *déjeuner*,
  And the solemn rent in arrears!) —
We laughed on the Champs Elysées,
  In the soft blue afternoons,
And I told you of my pictures,
  And you hummed your little tunes.

When we were poor in Paris,
  The days were lean and long;
Yet life was one bright Turner,
  And love an old French song.
I daubed with crimson brushes,
  You trilled, and reached high C;
But no one bought my pictures;
  You only sang — for me.

Alas! those days have vanished,
  The shifter's changed the scene;
We're rich in wild Manhattan,
  And own our limousine.
But when the Maytime madness
  Comes swinging down the year,

O, to be poor in Paris
With you again, my dear!
CHARLES HANSON TOWNE

LIGHT LOVE

THE love that is not quite love —
  Ah! let us be kind to it!
For it bears a touch of the dream above,
  The passion exquisite.

The love that is not quite love,
  But only a fleeting thing,
Like the wraith of rain in an Autumn lane,
  Or the thought of an unborn Spring.

The love that is not quite love,
  The careless, happy glance;
But deep in its heart it holds a part
  Of glamour and high romance.

A flash from the fire divine,
  A glimpse of the page unwrit;
The youthful love that is not quite love —
  Ah! let us be kind to it!
CHARLES HANSON TOWNE

233

AFTER ALL

WHEN, after all, you come to Love and lay
Your weary hands within his hands and say,
   'Love, thou art best!' how can you know that then
He will not laugh and turn his face away?

When, after many conflicts, your proud heart,
Seamed with old scars, would take Love's quiet part —
   Ah, to make fair that place for him again
Which of all Love's physicians has the art?

ARTHUR UPSON

SINCE WE SAID GOOD-BYE

KISSED we not and said good-bye?
   Then why wilt thou haunt me thus
With thine eyes in all my dreams
   Making night-time luminous?
Art thou haunted, dear, as I,
Since we kissed and said good-bye?

Had we kissed not, parting so,
   This were only just in thee;
Had we kissed and said no word
   Thou hadst right to torture me;
But thou knowest, well as I,
First we kissed, then said good-bye!

That good-byes may last too long —
   Is it this thine eyes would tell?

Or do they reproaching plead
   Kisses do not last so well?
Art thou lonelier than I
Since we kissed and said good-bye?

ARTHUR UPSON

TO LOVERS

LAD, will you draw the lightning down,
And pluck the morning-star from the sky,
To light a fire on your hearthstone
That a wilful girl may sit thereby?

Maid, will you harness the eagle's wings
And bit the jaws of the restless foam,
And change the cry of the gypsy wind
For the click of a latch when your man comes home?

Swift and sure go the lonely feet,
And the single eye sees cold and true,
And the road that has room and to spare for one
May be sorely narrow for two —

Yet still they light their fire at the stars,
And still they bridle the chafing sea,
For the sake of a dream that has always been....
That will always be.

AMELIA JOSEPHINE BURR

ISLAND TEA

Not though I grow old and gray,
In my heart no longer gay,
Shall I forget the day
   Dorothy,
Island goddess young and fair,
With a Nereid's green-gold hair,
And a happy smiling air,
   Made the tea.

Fresh from her bath she came,
And her glowing face aflame,
Made the summer sunset tame
   At the close
Of the tranquil afternoon,
When the still air seemed to swoon,
And the silver sickle moon
   Swam in rose.

As each fragrant cup she drew
Of the lucent amber brew,
At the table set for two,
   O'er the cove,
She carefully slipped in
A slice of lemon thin,
Like a golden fish's fin,
   And a clove.

Radiant, divinely bright,
Shining lily sheathed in white,

236

She made each simple rite
    A magic spell,
That upon my senses crept,
Till it seemed as if I slept,
And Calypso's island kept
    Me chained well.

Young sorceress whose arts
Will soon ensnare all hearts,
And whose eyes will scatter darts
    Barbed with blisses,
In your isle with trophies set,
Taken in your beauty's net,
Prithee do not quite forget
    Your first Ulysses!

WILLIAM ASPENWALL BRADLEY

A MODERN LOCHINVAR

GRANDUNCLE used to beau, he said,
    A prim New England girl;
Her hair was flattened to her head,
    Without a wave or curl;
Her poplin frock was so severe
    That none, you may be sure,
Would ever guess the little dear
    Had quite a *bonne tournure.*

He said a chill about him closed
    Within her parlor door.

237

Upon a walnut stand reposed
   The works of Hannah More;
A dismal vase exposed to view
   A posy of dried grass;
Wax flowers of a sickly hue
   Pined in their house of glass.

A cold black-marble mantelpiece
   O'ertopped a chilly grate;
Straight haircloth chairs, like dumb police,
   Stood round the walls in state;
And hanging by a velvet cord,
   In a vast walnut frame,
Was Infant Samuel when the Lord
   Was calling him by name.

If things moved with uncommon verve,
   At just half-after-eight
A pippin cold as ice she'd serve
   Upon a frosty plate.
The family at stroke of nine
   Would punctually appear
And range itself in solemn line
   For solemn Christian cheer.

Yet something drew him thither still
   (Or so he used to say),
And from the parlor's deadly chill
   He bore the maid away.
'Of all the gals that bards have sung,
   New England gals are best,'

He always said — 'but pick 'em young
And take 'em further west!'

GEORGE S. BRYAN

ONCE ON A TIME

ONCE on a time, once on a time,
  Before the Dawn began,
There was a nymph of Dian's train
  Who was beloved of Pan;
Once on a time a peasant lad
  Who loved a lass at home;
Once on a time a Saxon king
  Who loved a queen of Rome.

The world has but one song to sing,
  And it is ever new;
The first and last of all the songs,
  For it is ever true;
A little song, a tender song,
  The only song it hath:
'There was a youth of Ascalon
  Who loved a girl of Gath.'

A thousand thousand years have gone,
  And æons still shall pass,
Yet shall the world forever sing
  Of him who loved a lass —
An olden song, a golden song,
  And sing it unafraid:

239

'There was a youth, once on a time,
Who dearly loved a maid.'

KENDALL BANNING

A SILLY SONG

WE brought the wagons home at dusk,
With corn in golden satin husk,
And full of flagons filled with musk
And musca and the muscatel.
We took them all to the shop to sell.

Oh, livelier than the malted hops
Are you, whose sparkle never drops;
Sweeter than all the grapes in shops,
Than grapes upon the muscat vine,
Than musk, O Flower of Muscadine!

LOUIS HOW

VALENTINE TO ONE'S WIFE

HEARTS and darts and maids and men,
    Vows and valentines are here.
Will you give yourself again,
    Love me for another year?

Those who give themselves forever,
    All contingencies to cover,
Know but once the kind and clever
    Strategies of loved and lover;

240

Rather let the year renew
     Rituals of happiness;
When the season comes to woo,
     Let me ask, and you say yes.

Love me for another year,
     Here is heaven enough to climb,
If we measure, now and here,
     Each delicious step of time.

                              JOHN ERSKINE

THE GOSSIP

HAVING little else to do,
     And given to imagination,
She can break a word in two
     And make it fit the situation.

Blowing on some cold desire,
     Or some passion long-forgotten,
She can make it flare like fire
     Touching pine-knot, or gun-cotton.

Just a pair of ears and eyes
     That moth-like hover round life's candle; —
Her drink is ever spiked with lies;
     Her food forever spiced with scandal.

                    JOHN RICHARD MORELAND

REMEMBRANCE

I HAD not noticed scarlet haw
Or copper leaf on elm or oak,
Until I crossed the dunes and saw
The wild gold of the artichoke.

Strange how for just a moment's space,
The summer breeze that idled there
Brought the lost beauty of her face,
The wind-blown tangle of bright hair.

JOHN RICHARD MORELAND

THE PRIEST IS COME AND THE CANDLES BURN

THE white moth is wooing his chosen mate,
The birds have a nest in the weed and fern,
But, love, you knock at my heart too late,
The Priest is come and the candles burn.

Where were you, love, when the morning was heavy
with mating,
And in life's noontime before vivid dreams had departed?
Why did you tarry when twilight was weary with
waiting?
Lo, now it is midnight... pale sleep-time... and I am
chill-hearted.

The moon-flower bends with the moth's frail weight,

The birds are asleep in the grass and fern,
But, love, you knock at my heart too late,
The Priest is come and the candles burn.

JOHN RICHARD MORELAND

THE COQUETTE

SHE loves me and she loves me not,
    According to her whim;
For when another's on the spot
    Her love is all for him.

But I've been told a double cure:
    I'll simply let her be
And care no more, until I'm sure
    Her love is all for me.

And then I'll care enough to say,
    'Go to him and him!
For I but loved you yesterday —
    According to your whim.'

But first I'll give her one more chance
    To prove her constancy,
For, O, I know it by her glance,
    Her love is all for me!

WITTER BYNNER

THE SKEPTIC

WHAT shall I do, who may not be
    Beside you nor away?
Away I crave you, but, dear me,
    I doubt you if I stay —

Yes, doubt you with your equal eyes
    Of knowledge and of youth —
Your lovely wonders must be lies...
    And yet they may be truth!

Too hopeful not to come and see,
    Too skeptical to stay,
What shall I do who may not be
    Beside you nor away!

                    WITTER BYNNER

TO NO ONE IN PARTICULAR

LOCATE your love, you lose your love;
    Find her you look away....
Though mine I never quite discern,
    I trace her every day.

She has a thousand presences,
    As surely seen and heard
As birds that hide behind a leaf
    Or leaves that hide a bird.

Single your love, you lose your love,
  You cloak her face with clay;
Now mine I never quite discern —
  And never look away.

WITTER BYNNER

BEYOND RATHKELLY

As I went over the Far Hill,
  Just beyond Rathkelly, —
Och, to be on the Far Hill
  O'er Newtonstewart Town!
As I went over the Far Hill,
  With Marget's daughter Nellie,
The night was up and the moon was out,
  And a star was falling down.

As I went over the Far Hill,
  Just beyond Rathkelly, —
Och, to be on the Far Hill
  Above the Bridge o' Moyle!
As I went over the Far Hill,
  With Marget's daughter Nellie,
I made a wish before the star
  Had fallen in the Foyle.

As I went over the Far Hill,
  Just beyond Rathkelly, —
Och, to be on the Far Hill
  With the hopes that I had then!

As I went over the Far Hill,
I wished for little Nellie,
And if a star were falling now
I'd wish for her again.

FRANCIS CARLIN

THE POOR MAN

WITH an inexpensive jennet,
And a creel upon a cart,
And a cabin where a linnet
Often sings to break his heart;
It may sound a trifle funny,
But the truth I here declare:
Faith, 'tis not for want of money
That I'm not a millionaire.

All the silver in my pocket,
When I'm coming from the town,
Couldn't buy a copper locket
For to match a muslin gown;
But I've heard of golden coffers
Stated in a marriage plan,
So 'tis not for want of offers
That I'm not a wealthy man.

There's a party near the village
Who would make a likely match
For, with land too good for tillage,
Any woman is a catch;

But the matches and their makers
 Can go off to other scenes,
Since 'tis not for lack of acres
 That I'm not a man of means.

For the gold in Wicklow's ditches
 And the land of Louth, to me,
Would be only empty riches
 Wanting Nora MacNamee;
But that rose is full of honey
 Which a neighbor's bride shall wear,
So 'tis not for want of money
 That I'm not a millionaire.

FRANCIS CARLIN

AS TO EYES

LADY, better bards than I,
 Poets of an elder day,
Seemed to love to versify
 On 'her eyes,' or blue or gray.

'Tis an oft-recurrent theme
 For the bards who rhapsodize;
Not a one but used to dream
 Of the loveliness of eyes.

Shelley, Tennyson and Keats,
 Swinburne, Byron, Moore and Burns —
All had visual conceits,
 All had various optic yearns.

Far from me to minimize
   Elder, better bards, except
This: they spoke of ladies' eyes
   Haunting them what time they slept.

Envy I those troubadours,
   I am such a hopeless thrall,
Lady, when I think of yours,
   I — I cannot sleep at all.

FRANKLIN P. ADAMS

YOU AND I

OVER the hills, where the pine-trees grow,
   With a laugh to answer the wind at play.
Why do I laugh? I do not know,
   But you and I once passed this way.

Down in the hollow now white with snow
   My heart is singing a song today.
Why do I sing? I do not know,
   But you and I were here in May.

THOMAS S. JONES, JR.

MY SOUL IS LIKE A GARDEN–CLOSE

MY soul is like a garden-close
   Where marjoram and lilac grow,
   Where soft the scent of long ago
Over the border lightly blows.

Where sometimes homing winds at play
    Bear the faint fragrance of a rose —
    My soul is like a garden-close
Because you chanced to pass my way.

THOMAS S. JONES, JR.

FICKLENESS

I LOVED.... I lost.... 'The very world,'
    Thought I, 'must cease to be;
June finds no pleasure in her rose,
    Since She no more loves me!'

But when I saw the world still glad
    With sun and flower and rain,
That June had not forgot her rose —
    I straightway loved again.

HARRY KEMP

PRITHEE, STRIVE NOT

PRITHEE, strive not to remember
    Ancient love burnt out and dead;
Blow not on the blackened ember, —
    Ash will ne'er again give red.

Lift the latch — another lover
    Waits upon thy kiss without;
All the old things have gone over
    That the heart was mad about.

HARRY KEMP

PIERROT

Pierrot stands in the garden
  Beneath a waning moon,
And on his lute he fashions
  A fragile silver tune.

Pierrot plays in the garden,
  He thinks he plays for me,
But I am quite forgotten
  Under the cherry tree.

Pierrot plays in the garden,
  And all the roses know
That Pierrot loves his music, —
  But I love Pierrot.

SARA TEASDALE

FOUR WINDS

'Four winds blowing through the sky,
You have seen poor maidens die,
Tell me then what I shall do
That my lover may be true.'
Said the wind from out the south,
'Lay no kiss upon his mouth,'
And the wind from out the west,
'Wound the heart within his breast,'
And the wind from out the east,
'Send him empty from the feast,'

And the wind from out the north,
'In the tempest thrust him forth;
When thou art more cruel than he,
Then will Love be kind to thee.'

SARA TEASDALE

THE LOOK

Strephon kissed me in the spring,
   Robin in the fall,
But Colin only looked at me
   And never kissed at all.

Strephon's kiss was lost in jest,
   Robin's lost in play,
But the kiss in Colin's eyes
   Haunts me night and day.

SARA TEASDALE

LOVE AMONG THE CLOVER

'If you dare,' she said,
And oh, her breath was clover-sweet!
Clover nodded over her,
Her lips were clover-red.
Blackbirds fluted down the wind,
The bobolinks were mad with joy,
The wind was playing in her hair,
And 'If you dare,' she said.

251

Clover billowed down the wind
Far across the happy fields,
Clover on the breezy hills
Leaned along the skies,
And all the nodding clover heads
And little clouds with silver sails,
And all the heaven's dreamy blue
Were mirrored in her eyes.

Her laughing lips were clover-red
When long ago I kissed her there
And made for one swift moment all
My heaven and earth complete.
I've loved among the roses since,
And love among the lilies now,
But love among the clover...
Her breath was clover-sweet.

O wise, wise-hearted boy and girl
Who played among the clover bloom
I think I was far wiser then
Than now I dare to be.
For I have lost that Eden now,
I cannot find my Eden now,
And even should I find it now,
I've thrown away the key.

ODELL SH

252

A VIRGINAL

No, no! Go from me. I have left her lately.
I will not spoil my sheath with lesser brightness,
For my surrounding air has a new lightness;
Slight are her arms, yet they have bound me straitly
And left me cloaked as with a gauze of æther;
As with sweet leaves; as with a subtle clearness.
Oh, I have picked up magic in her nearness
To sheathe me half in half the things that sheathe her.

No, no! Go from me. I have still the flavour,
Soft as spring wind that's come from birchen bowers.
Green come the shoots, aye, April in the branches,
As winter's wound with her sleight hand she staunches,
Hath of the trees a likeness of the savour:
As white their bark, so white this lady's hours.

EZRA POUND

THE EMBARRASSED AMORIST

I CANNOT choose between them now,
  And yet I have to choose.
A hand, a foot, a child-like brow,
  Enrapture me.... But whose?

I seem to have no will at all,
  Only a stubborn need;
Blindly I follow beauty's call
  Wherever it may lead.

I run to Anna's soothing arms,
    Knowing that peace is best —
And then the thought of Lucy's charms
    Provokes me out of rest.

I tear myself, but I am loath
    To tear my soft chains free.
How can I strike at one, when both
    Seem so wrapped up in me?

And though I know what should be done,
    I know what I cannot do....
It's heaven to be in love with one
    But hell to be loved by two!

LOUIS UNTERMEYER

THE WISE WOMAN

His eyes grow hot, his words grow wild;
    He swears to break the mold and leave her.
She smiles at him as at a child
    That's touched with fever.

She smoothes his ruffled wings, she leans
    To comfort, pamper and restore him;
And when he sulks or scowls, she preens
    His feathers for him.

He hungers after stale regrets,
    Nourished by what she offers gaily;

And all he thinks he never gets
    She feeds him daily.

He lusts for freedom; cries how long
    Must he be bound by what controlled him!
Yet he is glad the chains are strong,
    And that they hold him.

She knows he feels all this, but she
    Is far too wise to let him know it;
He needs to nurse the agony
    That suits a poet.

He laughs to see her shape his life,
    As she half-coaxes, half-commands him;
And groans it's hard to have a wife
    Who understands him.

LOUIS UNTERMEYER

BALLADE OF MY LADY'S BEAUTY

Squire Adam had two wives, they say,
    Two wives had he, for his delight,
He kissed and clypt them all the day,
    And clypt and kissed them all the night.
    Now Eve like ocean foam was white
And Lilith roses dipped in wine,
    But though they were a goodly sight
No lady is so fair as mine.

255

To Venus some folk tribute pay
    And Queen of Beauty she is hight,
And Sainte Marie the world doth sway
    In cerule napery bedight.
    My wonderment these twain invite,
Their comeliness it is divine,
    And yet I say in their despite,
No lady is so fair as mine.

Dame Helen caused a grievous fray,
    For love of her brave men did fight,
The eyes of her made sages fey
    And put their hearts in woful plight.
    To her no rhymes will I indite,
For her no garlands will I twine,
    Though she be made of flowers and light
No lady is so fair as mine.

ENVOY

Prince Eros, Lord of lovely might
    Who on Olympus dost recline,
Do I not tell the truth aright?
    No lady is so fair as mine.

                    JOYCE KILMER

THE HOUR OF THE MORNING-STAR

BECAUSE in the hour of the morning-star
    I needs must lie awake,
I take the hour of the morning-star
    To sing in, for her sake.

Then, when the brows of the dawn are pale
    And the mouth of the morning meek,
The young day-star hangs sweetly there,
    Like the mole upon her cheek.

In the half-light, 'twixt night and light,
    These dreams of her I make,
Ere all the heaven of all the light
    Kiss all my love awake.

JOHN HALL WHEELOCK

IMPRISONED

In my song my love is prisoned
    As a bird within a cage.
Your lips only may unlock him
    From the prison of the page.

If you hear within his singing,
    With your lips you may unbar
The gold gate that shines between you,
    As the twilight frees her star

That the day but reimprisons:
    — He will seek another cage,
In your heart, dear, in your breast, dear,
    Fluttering upward from the page.

JOHN HALL WHEELOCK

257

THE LAST NIGHT

HADN'T we better rise and go
    Down to the wood so ashen white?
And you will give me a kiss I know
    Since this is our last night.

I will give you a kiss indeed,
    A kiss for this and a kiss for that!
And maybe a kiss to fill your need —
    So go and get your hat.

This place is best of all, I think,
    With the white star-blossoms in the grass,
And a whip-poor-will may come to drink,
    But never a body pass.

This place is well enough, indeed,
    To bind my soul and senses quite,
For I shall never again be freed
    From the kiss I give tonight.

                                    ORRICK JOHNS

HUGH, THE CARTER, TARRIES

TONIGHT, the country wine was clear
And you were deft to hand it;
Yet now you lie beside me, dear,
You scarcely understand it.
You brought a leaf of lavender,
And I blew out the candle....

You do not breathe or yield or stir,
With mystery to handle.

I know, my sweet, that day will come
And bring a gray reminder,
Yet in the flying hours of night
You need but be the kinder.
I know that every burnished star
Will fade to ash above me,
Yet... nestle to me as you are,
And while you love me, love me.

I know that I must rise at dawn
To take the dusty highway;
And you must stay behind, or go,
But never travel my way.
There is no seal of love to bind,
(No touch of mine has bound you)...
Perhaps another night will find
Another's arms around you.

But now tonight the fire lies still
Upon the rosy ceiling,
Across the moonlit window-sill
The jasmine scent is stealing.
Your golden hair about my face
The while you lean above me;
Tonight, tonight, dear, draw me close...
And while you love me, love me.

WILLARD WATTLES

A DISCOVERY OF NO IMPORTANCE

THE memory of one day
Lost in the lilt of laughter
Sweetens twenty years
That solemnly come after.

The memory of one night
And touch of white hands clinging
Can fling a noose of light
And fill all time with singing.

WILLARD WATTLES

THE DEVIL IS DYING

OH, it is good to camp with the spirit!
Oh, it is jaunty to walk with the mind!
When the heart sees all the future to share it,
Knowing the road that stretches behind.

Courage, my comrade, the devil is dying!
Here's the warm sun and a cloud scudding free;
The touch of your hand is too near for denying,
And laughter's a tavern sufficient for me.

Hang your old hat on the smoke-mellowed rafter,
Strike an old song on your crazy guitar;
Hey, hustle, old lady, it's heaven we're after —
God, but I'm glad we can be what we are!

WILLARD WATTLES

SONG

LOVE's on the highroad,
Love's in the byroad —
   Love's on the meadow, and Love's in the mart!
And down every byway
Where I've taken my way
   I've met Love a-smiling — for Love's in my heart!

DANA BURNET

THE MODERN WOMAN TO HER LOVER

I SHALL not lie to you any more,
   Flatter or fawn to attain my end —
I am what never has been before,
   Woman — and Friend.

I shall be strong as a man is strong,
   I shall be fair as a man is fair,
Hand locked in hand we shall pass along
   To a purer air:

I shall not drag at your bridle-rein,
   Knee pressed to knee shall we ride the hill;
I shall not lie to you ever again —
   Will you love me still?

MARGARET WIDDEMER

WARNING

As long as you never marry me, and I never marry you,
There's nothing on earth that we cannot say and no-
      thing we cannot do —
The flames lift up from our blowing hair, the leaves
      flash under our feet
When once in a year or a score of years our hands and
      our laughters meet!

For east and west through a sorry world we pass with
      our joy to sell,
And they that buy of our song and jest they praise us
      that we do well,
But few can sell us the mirth they buy, and few be that
      know a song,
And for all of the praise of the kindly folk, their speeches
      are over-long.

But two of a trade, one always hears, might get in each
      other's way,
And you might be wanting to sing, God wot, when I
      desired to play,
(Oh, it's rather a danger with folks like us and our
      sparks that are flying free)
But I never, never must marry you, and you never
      must marry me!

Now when we take breath from songs at last, to be what
      the rest call dead,
They'll sigh, 'Ah, noble the songs they made, and noble
      the jests they said!'

And they will inscribe on our monuments regret that
    our day is done —
But we will be off in an excellent place, and having most
    excellent fun —

Oh, very proud from a golden cloud you'll stride in your
    crown and wings,
Till you hear my little earthly giggle behind my gold
    harp-strings;
And you'll toss your gilt theorbo down on the nearest
    star or moon,
And carry me off on a comet's back for a long, wild
    afternoon;

And while we're lashing the comet up till it misses St.
    Michael's Way,
And laugh to think how the seraphs blink, and what the
    good saints will say,
We'll heave a little sigh of content — or a wistful one,
    maybe —
To know that I never can marry you, and you never can
    marry me!

MARGARET WIDDEMER

IF YOU SHOULD TIRE OF LOVING ME

If you should tire of loving me
  Some one of our far days,
Then never start to hide your heart
  Or cover thought with praise.

For every word you would not say
  Be sure my heart has heard,
So go from me all silently
  Without a kiss or word;

For God must give you happiness...
  And, oh, it may befall
In listening long to Heaven-song
  I may not care at all!

MARGARET WIDDEMER

NEVER WILL YOU HOLD ME

Never will you hold me
  With puddings and cake,
Or even the threat
  Of a heart to break.

Never will you hold me
  With knife, fork and spoon
As long as the road lies
  Under the moon.

Nor phantoms at fireside
  With grief in the room,
Nor obvious candles
  To jewel the gloom.

But a song satyr-footed,
  A mood of gowns of gold,

264

And laughter like a wine-cup —
   These things hold.

A song within a song
   And eyes upon the door —
And you will always hold me
   One day more.

CHARLES DIVINE

LET OUR LOVE BE

BELOVED, let our love be quite
Intense and splendid, but polite,
That in the hour of parting, we
May end the matter pleasantly.

Since the foredoomed farewell is core
Of all the mortal evermore,
Let us not mar with present fret
The gracious sequel of regret.

Rather, my little love, let me
Your guide for future lovers be,
Whose pleasure now is sometimes fraught
With envy of the men who taught.

SAMUEL HOFFENSTEIN

OF A CHILD THAT HAD FEVER

I BID you, mock not Eros
    Lest Eros mock with you.
His is a hot distemper
    That hath no fever-few.

Love, like a child in sickness,
    Brilliant, languid, still,
In fiery weakness lying,
    Accepts, and hath no will.

See, in that warm dispassion
    Less grievance than surprise,
And pitiable brightness
    In his poor wondering eyes.

Oh, delicate heat and madness,
    Oh, lust unnerved and faint:
Sparkling in veins and fibres,
    Division and attaint!

I bid you, mock not Eros;
    He knows not doubt or shame,
And, unaware of proverbs,
    The burnt child craves the flame.

CHRISTOPHER MORLEY

266

DEAD ENCHANTRESS

As well be dead as Egypt is
    And stone beneath my lips, as well
Be dust already if each kiss
    Is guarded by a sentinel.

You have no pity; Lilith might
    Have given rapture in your stead;
You walk the battlements of night
    A moon-queen unaccompanied.

Though no recorded hours mark
    A change in what has been before,
I whip my horses up the dark
    And bring my chariot to your door.

                    HAROLD VINAL

THURSDAY

AND if I loved you Wednesday,
    Well, what is that to you?
I do not love you Thursday —
    So much is true.

And why you come complaining
    Is more than I can see.
I loved you Wednesday, — yes — but what
    Is that to me?

            EDNA ST. VINCENT MILLAY

THE PHILOSOPHER

AND what are you that, missing you,
  I should be kept awake
As many nights as there are days
  With weeping for your sake?

And what are you that, missing you,
  As many days as crawl
I should be listening to the wind
  And looking at the wall?

I know a man that's a braver man
  And twenty men as kind,
And what are you, that you should be
  The one man in my mind?

Yet women's ways are witless ways,
  As any sage will tell, —
And what am I, that I should love
  So wisely and so well?

EDNA ST. VINCENT MILLAY

TO THE NOT IMPOSSIBLE HIM

How shall I know, unless I go
  To Cairo and Cathay,
Whether or not this blessed spot
  Is blest in every way?

Now it may be, the flower for me
  Is this beneath my nose;
How shall I tell, unless I smell
  The Carthagenian rose?

The fabric of my faithful love
  No power shall dim or ravel
While I stay here, — but, oh, my dear,
  If I should ever travel!

EDNA ST. VINCENT MILLAY

INCURABLE

AND if my heart be scarred and burned
The safer, I, for all I learned;
The calmer, I, to see it true
That ways of love are never new —
The love that sets you daft and dazed
Is every love that ever blazed;
The happier, I, to fathom this:
A kiss is every other kiss.
The reckless vow, the lovely name,
When Helen walked, were spoke the same;
The weighted breast, the grinding woe,
When Phaon fled, were ever so.
Oh, it is sure as it is sad
That any lad is every lad,
And what's a girl, to dare implore
Her dear be hers forevermore?
Though he be tried and he be bold,

And swearing death should he be cold,
He'll run the path the others went....
But you, my sweet, are different.

DOROTHY PARKER

THE FALSE FRIENDS

THEY laid their hands upon my head,
They stroked my cheek and brow;
And time could heal a hurt, they said,
And time could dim a vow.

And they were pitiful and mild
Who whispered to me then,
'The heart that breaks in April, child,
Will mend in May again.'

Oh, many a mended heart they knew,
So old they were, and wise,
And little did they have to do
To come to me with lies.

Who flings me silly talk of May
Shall meet a bitter soul;
For June was nearly spent away
Before my heart was whole.

DOROTHY PARKER

TO A LADY

I WILL give to you diamonds and rubies
  And pearls in a golden crown;
For a smile of your grey eyes, lady,
  I will tumble a mountain down.

I will give to you garlands and roses,
  And fruit of the blossoming year,
Aye, song-books and poems and posies, —
  All these will I give you, dear.

I will give you my whole life's treasure,
  My flowers of dream and of art —
All things will I give to you, lady,
  Saving my heart.

JOHN MCCLURE

I GAVE MY LOVE

I GAVE my love to a wastrel
  With bonny autumn eyes,
He spent his days in foolish ways,
  But, oh, his heart was wise!

He flung my love to the wanton winds,
  And broke my heart in twain,
But, oh, would he come asking
  I'd give it him again!

LEXIE DEAN ROBERTSON

BATTERY PARK

BEHIND me lie the clumping streets,
Before, the brawling harbor lies;
But what of towns and what of fleets
With such a sun in such blue skies?
O, I could sit the whole day through,
My dear, my dear, and think of you!

Drowsy I watch with half an eye
The pigeons flutter, marveling
By two and two how close they fly,
How very close there, wing to wing.
O, I could sit the whole day long
And never hear a sound but song!

O, I could sit all day and hold
Your hand and feel your shoulder press
On mine and feel the sun enfold
Both in one flame of tenderness!
And since you do not love me, dear,
I am quite glad you are not here.

LEONARD CLINE

VOWS

WHEN lovers in the spring contend
Which one the fairest vow can say,
Speak bravely, lad, and in the end
Let each the score with kisses pay.

It is a game one could not choose
Whether 'twere best to win or lose.

Till no star shines that's shining now,
My dear, my dear, my troth I plight,
A lass may say, and a lad may vow
Till the dark prairie of the night
Blossom no more at dawn with blue,
My dear, my dear, I will love you.

But if she sigh upon that thought,
As my love did, let playing cease;
Be silent then as I was not
And pledge no more eternities,
Lad, lad! nor put your heart at stake,
As I did mine, lest it should break.

LEONARD CLINE

OF ROSES

I LOVE Love!
  And so I take
With quick hands
  The sure heart-break
That comes with love.
  A thorn may sting:
But isn't a rose
  A pretty thing?

MARY CAROLYN DAVIES

HONEYMOON

God built the earth
In seven:
In one day
You built heaven!

MARY CAROLYN DAVIES

TO A PRETTY WOMAN

You are a bugle blown for a weary bivouac;
　　You are the splendor of blood on burnished blades;
You are the west wind over a waste of sedges;
　　And you are a teak-wood cabinet filled with jades.

You are a topaz burned alone in a casket;
　　You are a glass to be drained and flung to the floor;
You are a reed that one might fashion for music;
　　You are a woman and you are nothing more.

But in your eyes are flames that flow in an opal;
　　Your mouth is hot as a roseleaf crushed from a rose;
You are the lie and the lure of all that is beauty...
　　And how I shall ever be quit of you now — God
　　　knows!

J. U. NICOLSON

WHEN AMARYLLIS BOWLS

My Amaryllis was not made
Like ordinary souls!
The Milky Way's her bowling green,
She uses moons for bowls.

She swings them down the starry sward
Till all of heaven wakes.
Oh! Truly she's no common girl —
She wins eternal stakes!

JOHN FARRAR

EPITHALAMION FOR AMARYLLIS

WELL-A-WAY; and so you pass,
Aye, you were a comely lass,
And I'll probably remember
Until, oh! at least September.
So here's farewell, Amaryllis,
Thank kind heaven that there still is
Youth and Hope, Aye — Let there be a
Fanfare for My DOROTHEA!

JOHN FARRAR

TWO

He is a leopard that changed each spot,
Sinuous, sensuous jungle-puss.
He is all creatures who were not —
Mythical, mad, anomalous.

275

She is the women who never were,
Before whose beauty the world grows dim....
'Now what on earth can he see in her?'
'And why in heaven does she pick him?'

RALPH CHENEY

HAD I NOT LOVED BEFORE

(With a Bow to Sir Richard Lovelace)

I COULD not love you, dear, so much
   Had I not loved before.
I thought that love was such — and — such.
   I find ours so much more.

I'd own more fealty to heart
   Than loyalty to you.
Through being false I've learned the art,
   My dear, of being true.

RALPH CHENEY

LADY IN A LIMOUSINE

THROUGH her lorgnette's disdainful glass
She looks upon earth's naked, patient grief.
Life's puppet tragedies emerge and pass
Like any aimless cloud or casual leaf.

She sits, a woman in an opera box,
Transparent china on a lofty shelf,

And does not know that this poor world she mocks
Contains no sadder object than herself.

LUCIA TRENT

SOCIETY WOMAN

HER feet press down the velvet ways
Of carpets and her hands are cool
On satin pillows. All her days
Are still-born shadows in a pool.

How pitiful her unconcern,
For what can these smooth years unroll
To one, who lives within the stern
And barren attic of her soul?

LUCIA TRENT

WHAT DOES IT MATTER NOW

WHAT does it matter now
That April's been and gone
And not a star is left
To pin a dream upon?

And not a road is left
To wander until Day
Comes streaming down the east
And bears our dreams away.

What does it matter now
If all loveliness

277

Prove fleeting as a song
Or a lost caress?

For I have met your eyes
And I have kissed your brow;
O wonderful and wise,
What does it matter now?

SYDNEY KING RUSSELL

POSSIBLY

HE wore a frock coat
    And a silk hat.
He wore a gray tie —
    It might have been that.

I could hear his bitter voice
    From where I sat.
I could see his bitter smile —
    It might have been that.

A nice man to listen to
    And to look at.
He never glanced my way —
    It *might* have been that.

ELSPETH MACDUFFIE O'HALLORAN

FORECAST

He has told me more than once
  That I'm really clever.
She will be a darling dunce
  He will love forever.

He has praised the songs I sing,
  Like a gallant fellow.
She will be a little thing
  With hair of spun yellow.

He admired my bitterness,
  Lashing life with whips.
He will wait to hear her 'yes'
  Whispered by shy lips.

ELSPETH MACDUFFIE O'HALLORAN

BUDGET

We could hang my Chartres upon a lamplit wall.
We could put your brasses on a table in the hall.
We could put my Morley where the sun would strike
    the blue,
And I think your heavy chair is big enough for two.

We could put my curtains in the window to the west.
We could put your Chinese rug wherever you like best.
We'd write all the morning and talk all afternoon,
And there will be a fire-escape for looking at the moon.

ELSPETH MACDUFFIE O'HALLORAN

TO ONE WHO SAID ME NAY

This much the gods vouchsafe today:
  That we two lie in clover,
Watching the heavens dip and sway,
  With galleons sailing over.

This much is granted for an hour:
  That we are young and tender,
That I am bee and you are flower,
  Honey-mouthed and swaying slender.

This sweet of sweets is ours now:
  To wander through the land,
Plucking an apple from its bough
  To toss from hand to hand.

No thing is certain, joy nor sorrow,
  Except the hour we know it;
Oh, wear my heart today; tomorrow
  Who knows where the winds will blow it?

                              COUNTEE CULLEN

QUERY

How delicate a thing it is!
Why, I could not say —
It has no name, it has no voice,
It only has a way.

Subtle as the hush of leaves,
Protective as a glove,
I cannot call it friendship, yet
I cannot call it love.

I'm sure we'd never wish to wed,
I hope we'll never part —
How strange is this, which has no end
Yet never seemed to start!

VIRGINIA LAWRENCE

WISDOM

LAST night your heart was mine.
This I could avow.
You did not speak — and yet I knew
Somehow.

Tonight, and all is changed.
You are another's now.
You thought to hide it, but I knew
Somehow.

VIRGINIA LAWRENCE

INDEX OF FIRST LINES

283

285

288

INDEX OF TITLES

296

298

INDEX OF AUTHORS

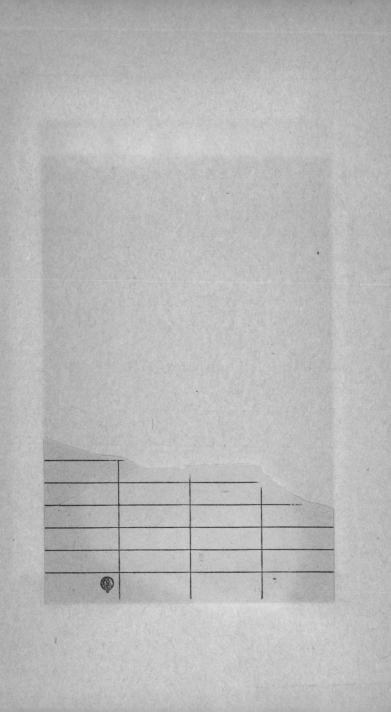